Coordinator's Handbook

This Handbook is written for numeracy coordinators in schools which use STEPS as their main resource for mathematics. The main aims of the Handbook are to:

■ provide general information about the Framework for Teaching Mathematics which had to be taken into account in planning the content of this Handbook;

■ show how STEPS can be used to support the learning objectives and styles of teaching and learning required by the Framework;

■ suggest procedures for medium- and short-term planning which show how STEPS might be linked to the relevant learning objectives in the Framework for any year group;

■ provide other information relevant to planning for the National Numeracy Strategy and the Framework;

■ provide a correlation guide which cross-references units within the STEPS Handbooks to the objectives in the Framework for each year group R to Y6.

Coordinator's notes

Some Copymasters which are suitable for making OHTs are included for in-service training. These are accompanied by notes which expand the points on the Copymaster, to support the coordinator or in-service leader.

Any part of this booklet may be reproduced for training purposes within the purchasing school.

Contents

STEPS
MATHEMATICS

Numeracy
Co-ordinator's
Handbook

Using **STEPS** with
the Numeracy Strategy
and the Framework for
Teaching Mathematics

Anne Woodman

Acknowledgement
The publisher would like to thank Janine Blinco for her contribution to the exemplar lesson plans found in Section 3.

Published by Collins Educational
An imprint of HarperCollins*Publishers* Ltd
77-85 Fulham Palace Road
London W6 8JB

First published 1999

British Library Cataloguing in Publication Data
A catalogue record for this book is available from the British Library.

Series Editor: Anne Woodman
Edited by Gaynor Spry
Designed by Neil Adams, Grasshopper Design Company
Illustrated by Roy Mitchell

Printed in Great Britain by Martins the Printers, Berwick-Upon-Tweed

Introduction to the Framework

The National Numeracy Strategy and the Framework for Teaching Mathematics

Coordinator's notes
This and the following page expand the headings on CM1 on page 10 and can be used as a prompt for the coordinator to talk through the key points.

Background

The National Numeracy Project was set up in 1996 in response to inspection, test and research evidence which pointed to a need to improve standards of numeracy. Its aim is to help to ensure that 75% of all 11 year olds achieve Level 4 or above in the National Curriculum tests for mathematics by 2002.

The Framework for Teaching Mathematics is part of the materials produced by the project and is intended to be used for day-to-day reference by class teachers. It sets out the progression required by pupils each year from Reception to Year 6 with a view to achieving this aim.

The proposals in the report from the Numeracy Task Force, The Implementation of the National Numeracy Strategy, build on the good practice of the National Numeracy Project.

The National Curriculum Order is a statutory document stating what must be taught during a key stage. The Framework is not a statutory document but recommends a method for implementing the Order for KS1 and KS2.

Key points from the Introduction to the Framework

- The Framework provides guidance to supplement the National Curriculum Order which describes what must be taught in each key stage. It is also compatible with the proposals for the revised National Curriculum.

- The Framework, through Yearly Teaching Programmes setting out learning objectives for each mathematical topic, illustrates how mathematics can be planned and taught in each year from Reception to Year 6.

- A Yearly Teaching Programme (Summary of objectives) is provided for each year group and each objective should be covered at least once in that year.

- Some key objectives for each year group have been identified. These are listed separately and also emboldened in the Yearly Teaching Programme. Teachers should give priority to these when planning and assessing pupils' progress.

- Each Yearly Teaching Programme is accompanied by suggested/optional templates to help teachers plan work on a half-termly or termly basis to give suitable emphasis to numeracy. Time is built into these for half-termly assessing and reviewing.

- Supplements of examples follow which illustrate what pupils should know, understand and be able to do by the end of the year for each objective.

- Parents are encouraged to help their children to become numerate.

Teaching time

- Each child is expected to have a daily mathematics lesson of about 45 minutes in KS1 and 50 to 60 minutes in KS2.

- The teacher needs to plan for direct teaching and interactive oral work with the whole class and groups.

- There is an emphasis on mental calculation.

- Time should be found in other subjects for pupils to use and apply their numeracy skills.

Direct teaching

- Teaching should be based on the objectives in the Framework and direct teaching focused to attain the objectives for that lesson.

- Teaching should include elements of demonstration, explanation, questioning, discussion, evaluation of pupil's responses and directing children's progress.

Classroom organisation

- All pupils in Years 1 to 6 should work on mathematics at the same time for each lesson to establish common routines and patterns of working and to secure a balance between whole-class and group teaching.

- Each new unit of work is started with the whole class but children can then be grouped by ability in three or four groups to allow for a controlled degree of differentiation.

- At least one and possibly two groups should be targeted each day for direct teaching to provide guidance and discussion focused on their particular work and ability.

- Teaching should secure good progress by all children in the class and minimise the gap in attainment between the most and least able pupils.

- Pupils need to know what is expected of them in the time available, how to obtain and replace resources, agreed procedures for what to do if they finish early, get stuck etc. before asking an adult for help.

A typical lesson

■ A typical lesson is structured in this way:

Part of lesson	Time allocated	Type of work
oral work and mental calculation	5 to 10 minutes	whole class work: rehearsing and sharpening skills: counting, mental strategies, instant recall of +, −, × and ÷ facts every day
the main teaching activity	35 to 40 minutes	teaching and learning activities: work with whole class, groups, pairs or individuals
the plenary to round off the lesson	10 to 15 minutes	work with the whole class: reviewing progress, clarifying misconceptions, summarising, setting homework etc.

Coordinator's notes
CM2 (p.11) provides more detailed information about the structure of a typical lesson.

■ This structure can be varied to suit the lesson's objectives but, overall, there should be a high proportion of work with the whole class.

Differentiation

■ Although the main aim is to keep as many of the children as possible working on the same objectives, differentiated activities may be necessary for older or mixed-age classes.

■ The number of groups differentiated by ability should be manageable, e.g. three ability groups (with the largest 'middle' group possibly sitting at two tables but being brought together for targeted teaching).

■ When questions are asked, these might vary in difficulty to suit the range of ability, with, for example, the least-able children being asked questions appropriate to their ability.

■ The whole-class introduction to the main teaching activity might be shorter for the high-attainers with this group being set work to get on with whilst the introduction is extended for the middle-attainers and further extended for the low-attainers.

■ During the main activity, three differentiated activities might be planned around the main theme with a challenge set for the high-attainers, appropriate work set for the middle-attainers and less demanding work for the low-attainers.

■ Mixed-age classes might be reorganised into year groups for the daily mathematics lesson but they should still be taught the same topic at the same time by the teacher choosing objectives from the programmes for each year group.

■ Very small schools with three or more year groups in a class may need to organise groups (preferably no more than five) by ability rather than by year group but still base work on the same topic.

■ Some schools might organise ability sets for mathematics but this alone does not help to close the gap in attainment across a year group. Strategies for ensuring the transfer of pupils between sets are vital if setting is to be successful.

■ High-attaining pupils might be extended through group activities set in the main activity, extra challenges set towards the end of a topic or through more demanding homework. Schools may also make special arrangements so that this group moves more quickly through the objectives.

■ The Framework also gives guidance on supporting children with special needs and EAL pupils, and how classroom assistants can be used to support these pupils.

Resources

■ The Framework recommends essential resources and how these might be used. These include:

  • an OHP or flip chart for demonstrations, a black or white board;
  • various wall and desktop number lines, wall number squares etc;
  • a set of digit cards 0 to 9 for individual pupil use;
  • a range of pupil material for written work from different sources;
  • small equipment for each group, e.g. dice, counters, interlocking cubes;
  • a basic calculator for older pupils.

> **Coordinator's notes**
> *CM3 on pages 12–16 provides more detailed information about resources recommended by the Framework. These will assist in a school audit.*

Assessment

■ The Framework requires regular assessments of pupils' progress and systematic recording of this.

■ Forms of assessment include:

  • informal tests of mental recall and mental calculation;
  • the use of the supplement of examples to plan assessment activities for two days at the end of each half-term;
  • individual target-setting with each pupil once a term;
  • teacher evaluation of the termly plan to review what has been taught and what remains to be learned;
  • assessing and recording each child's progress at least once a year against National Curriculum level descriptions.

Planning

■ The Framework for Teaching Mathematics comprises:

  • a Yearly Teaching Programme for each year group, covering all relevant aspects of the National Curriculum for mathematics;
  • planning templates to help plan lessons for each term;
  • supplements of examples for each year group.

■ The supplements exemplify the range of what pupils should know and be able to do by the end of the year and are linked to the National Curriculum.

■ The Framework's five strands incorporate the Programmes of Study for Number, Handling Data, Measures and Shape and Space for KS1 and KS2.

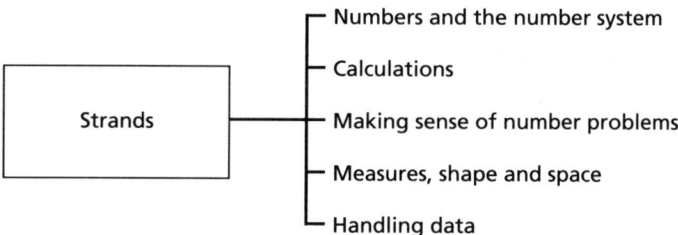

■ Each strand is broken down into topics, e.g. Numbers and the number system.

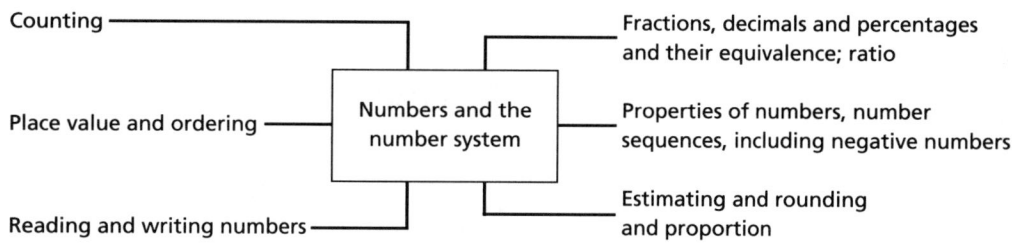

■ Each topic is broken down into objectives in the Yearly Teaching Programme (Summary of objectives), e.g. Rapid recall of number facts from the Calculations strand.

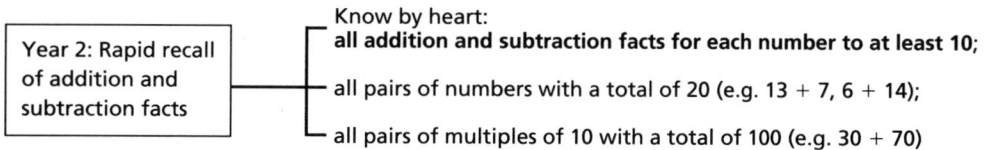

Note that the objective in bold type is a **key objective** and is deemed to be more critical than the others.

■ Teaching plans must cover all five strands and help children make linKSbetween them.

■ Ideas for children using and applying their mathematical knowledge are integrated into the Yearly Teaching Programme for each year group, e.g. in the Making sense of number problems strand.

■ Three levels of planning are needed to put the Framework into practice:

- **the Framework**   what has to be taught long-term;
- **medium-terms plans**   termly or half-termly plans with their main teaching objectives and when they are to be taught;
- **short-term plans**   weekly or fortnightly plans for five or ten lessons, including how pupils will be grouped and which groups will be targeted for teaching.

(This is dealt with in more detail in Section 3: Medium- and short-term planning from the Framework.)

■ Each class in the school is expected to engage in daily mathematics lessons based on the Framework.

The National Numeracy Strategy and the Framework

Key Points

■ Background

■ Teaching time

■ Direct teaching

■ Class organisation

■ A typical lesson

■ Differentiation

■ Resources

■ Assessment

■ Planning

Please note. These key points represent a summary of relevant information from the Introduction to the Framework. They are not a substitute for reading the whole of the Introduction, which is essential reading for every primary teacher.

A typical lesson

WHOLE CLASS   **5–10 MINUTES**

Introduction

- oral and mental work to rehearse and sharpen skills

WHOLE CLASS
GROUPS   **30–40 MINUTES**
PAIRS
INDIVIDUALS

Main activity

- clear objectives shared with pupils

- direct interactive teaching input

- practical and/or written work for pupils
  on the same theme for all the class

- if group work, usually differentiated at no more than
  three levels, with focused teaching of one or two
  groups for part of the time

- continued interaction and intervention

- misconceptions identified

WHOLE CLASS   **10–15 MINUTES**

Plenary

- feedback from children to identify progress and
  sort misconceptions

- summary of key ideas, what to remember

- links made to other work, discussion of next steps

- work set to do at home

Resources for the Framework

Whole class resources

■ **Board**

■ **Demonstration number lines: marked and unmarked**

    Y2   numbers to 100

    Y4   should be able to demonstrate negative numbers

    Y5/Y6 should be able to demonstrate fractions and decimals

■ **Washing line of numbers (adaptable, extendable)**

■ **Numbered carpet tiles (optional)**

■ **Floor or playground snakes (optional) with spaces numbered to 20 at least (R and Y1)**

■ **100-square: numbered and blank**

■ **OHP/OHP calculator**

■ **Base 10 materials/base 10 spike abaci**

■ **Digit cards 0–9 and symbol (+, −, ×, ÷) cards, at least A4 size**

Resources for the Framework

Children's resources

- Table-top number lines, marked and unmarked

  R/Y1 number tracks to 20 (spaces numbered)

  Y2 number lines to 100

  Y4 number lines to include negative numbers

  Y5/Y6 unmarked lines: decimals, fractions, percentages

- Digit cards or number fans 0–9 for each child

- Symbol cards: +, −, ×, ÷

- Places value cards, e.g.

| 400 | 80 | 7 | | 4 | 8 | 7 |

- Addition and subtraction cards for number bonds (appropriate to objectives)

- Calculators (Y5 and Y6)

Resources for the Framework

For each classroom group

- counters
- interlocking cubes
- wooden cubes
- pegs
- pegboards

- straws
- rulers
- coins
- dice
- dominoes

For each classroom

- assorted grid papers, especially square and 'dotty' square grids

- number games

- measuring equipment: length, mass, capacity, time etc.

- sets of shapes and construction kits

Resources for the Framework

ICT

- calculators (Y5 and Y6)

- OHT demonstration calculator

- computers with software to support:
  number patterns and sequences
  consolidation and practice of number skills
  estimating and comparing measures/angles
  problem-solving using screen turtles

- programmable robots

- audio-visual aids, e.g. tables, educational broadcasts, video film

Library

- interest books on mathematics

- mathematical dictionaries

Resources for the Framework

For 'Shape and Space'

■ 3-D shapes

■ 2-D shapes (including non-regular polygons)

■ modelling material for KS1

■ mosaic-type pattern building kits

■ Geostrips

■ pairs of compasses

■ pinboards

■ safety mirrors

■ computer programs

■ set squares

■ protractors (circular)

Planning: STEPS and the Framework

Effective planning

To provide an effective whole-school strategy for planning, implementing and monitoring the Framework, there is a need to consider four essential and connected issues: school policy, long-, medium- and short-term planning.

Planning issues: The Framework	Planning outcomes: The school
Policy National Numeracy Strategy and the Introduction to the Framework	**Policy statement:** setting out clearly the way in which the school intends to meet the requirements of the Numeracy Strategy and the Framework. The policy statement should: ■ guide the implementation of mathematics (including mental mathematics) throughout the school; ■ describe the purposes, nature and management of mathematics; ■ give guidance on parental involvement and homework; ■ be concise and unambiguous and worded so that monitoring criteria can be identified; ■ be understood and agreed by all the staff. Key points taken from the opening section in the Framework, 'Introducing the Framework', may assist schools in reviewing or rewriting their policy.
Long-term issues the Framework, setting out what you should teach long-term based on the National Curriculum	**School scheme of work:** the document of classroom practice, setting out the knowledge, skills and processes to be taught year-on-year, based on the Yearly Teaching Programmes in the Framework ■ To be effective, it must give clear guidance about the learning objectives to be covered and the range of teaching strategies to be adopted. ■ As each teacher creates medium- and short-term plans, the school can collate these to form the basis of their scheme of work for the whole school. ■ If these plans are eventually stored in an electronic form, they can be modified more easily.
Medium-term issues termly- or half-termly outlines of units of work drawn from the Yearly Teaching Programmes in the Framework	**School's own medium-term plans:** half-termly or termly plans drawn from the scheme of work ■ These need to take into account pace so that the objectives for the year can be covered. A common format needs to be agreed which takes into account what needs to be taught, the main learning objectives and when they will be taught. ■ At this stage, some of the learning objectives in the Framework may need to be broken down into less detailed objectives, i.e. focus on part of an objective. ■ Schools may wish to use the termly planning grids provided by the Framework.

Planning issues: The Framework	Planning outcomes: The school
Short-term plans weekly or fortnightly	**School's own short-term plans:** daily, weekly or fortnightly lesson plans in an agreed format, based on the structure of a typical lesson and developed in more detail from the medium-term plans. ■ Details should include what you will teach, what the pupils will do, resources, use of support staff, grouping arrangements, including identifying group(s) targeted for direct teaching, and key questions/ideas. ■ The supplement of examples in the Framework will inform short-term plans. ■ Evaluation of short-term plans will inform future half-termly or termly-plans.

Medium- and short-term planning

Procedures for medium- and short-term planning using the Framework in conjunction with STEPS are dealt with in detail in Section 3, 'Medium- and short-term planning from the Framework'.

> ### Coordinator's notes
> *The flowchart on CM4 (p.19) shows how the planning issues in this section connect with the monitoring, assessment and recording of pupils' progress. (A summary of the assessment arrangements recommended by the Framework is given on p.8 in Section 1.)*

Using the Framework to plan for mathematics

This flowchart shows how the planning issues connect with the monitoring, assessment and recording of pupils' progress.

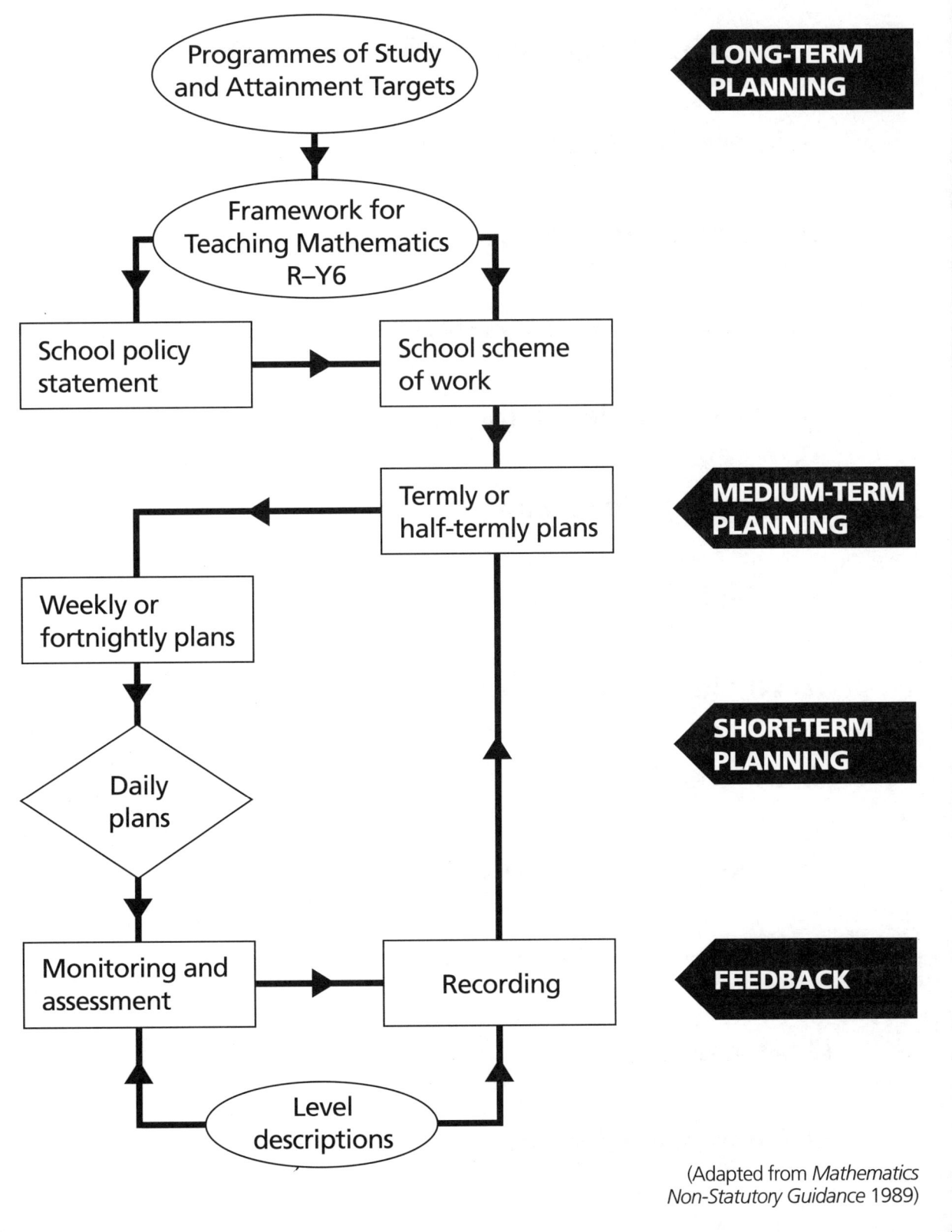

(Adapted from *Mathematics Non-Statutory Guidance* 1989)

STEPS Mathematics
and The Framework for Teaching Mathematics

Commonality of approach

1 Interactive, direct teaching

2 Clearly-defined objectives

3 Emphasis on mental calculation

4 Cross-curricular mathematics

5 Language development

6 A typical lesson

7 Whole class, group, paired and individual work

8 Differentiation

9 Links with the National Curriculum

10 Using and applying mathematics

11 Assessment

12 Parental involvement

Notes on CM5: STEPS Mathematics and The Framework for Teaching Mathematics

Commonality of approach

Coordinator's note
This and the following page expand the headings on CM5 (p.20) and may be used as a prompt for the coordinator to talk through the issues.

	The Framework	STEPS Mathematics
1	**Interactive, direct teaching** The teacher needs to plan for direct teaching and interactive oral work with the whole class and groups.	The STEPS approach is centred on teachers introducing the learning objectives through direct teaching to the whole class or to groups as appropriate. The Teachers' Handbooks are the key resource and STEPS has always recommended that pupil material is to be used only at the discretion of the teacher after direct teaching.
2	**Clearly-defined objectives** Teaching should be based on the objectives in the Framework and direct teaching focused to attain the objectives for that lesson.	Each Step has clearly defined objectives and the activities have been carefully chosen to cover the objectives with the help of direct teaching. Most of these objectives have a parallel in the Framework.
3	**Emphasis on mental calculation** There is an emphasis on mental calculation.	Mental calculation, including both recall of facts and strategies for calculation, are integrated throughout the Handbook.
4	**Cross-curricular mathematics** Time should be found in other subjects for pupils to use and apply their numeracy skills.	Most Steps include ideas for developing cross-curricular links or ideas for using and applying mathematics.
5	**Language development** Teaching should include elements of demonstration, explanation, questioning, discussion, evaluation of pupil's responses and the directing of children's progress.	STEPS places a high priority on the development of pupils' mathematical language. Each Step identifies key language on which the teacher should concentrate in demonstrations, explanations, discussions with the children and when asking open and closed questions.
6	**A typical lesson** A typical lesson contains these three elements: ■ oral work and mental calculation; ■ the main teaching activity; ■ a plenary session.	The activities in 'Detail' in each Step, written in lesson-plan format, combine direct exposition by the teacher, questions to ask and a main teaching activity. Many activities also have suggestions for mental mathematics or for rounding off the lesson.
7	**Whole class, group, paired and individual work** The main teaching activity should include work as a whole class, and will also include group, paired or individual work, whichever is the most appropriate.	Each Step suggests opportunities for whole class, group, paired and individual work. Suggestions are often made for children to work collaboratively.

		The Framework	STEPS Mathematics
8	**Differentiation**	During the main teaching activity, three differentiated activities might be planned around the main theme with a challenge set for the high-attainers, appropriate work set for the middle-attainers and less demanding work for the low-attainers.	In each Step, ideas for extending the high-ability children are suggested as extensions after most activities in 'Detail' and separately as 'Challenging activities'. Some suggestions are also made to assist children struggling with the learning objectives. Additionally, STEPS Differentiation Packs (to support each Step in the STEPS Handbooks from 3a onwards) offer further activities for the low-, middle- and high-ability children.
9	**Links with the National Curriculum**	The Framework incorporates the Programmes of Study for Number, Handling Data, Measures and Shape and Space for KS1 and KS2.	STEPS was written after the publication of the National Curriculum Orders and is based on the content of the Programmes of Study for KS1 and KS2. Each Step has been cross-referenced to the National Curriculum. Additionally, a chart in each Handbook shows, for each section of the relevant Programme of Study, a list of relevant Steps in each Handbook.
10	**Using and applying mathematics**	Using and applying is integrated throughout.	Every effort has been made to take into account the requirements of the Programme of Study for Using and Applying Mathematics throughout the Handbooks. Some aspects of this are explicitly identified in the objectives for a Step; at other times, using and applying is implicit. However, it is recognised that some of the required aspects cannot be catered for within a published resource, e.g. mathematics arising out a school's particular environment or curricular activities.
11	**Assessment**	The main focus of assessment in the Framework is through teachers making regular assessments of pupils' progress based on the year's learning objectives and particularly against the key objectives.	STEPS has adopted this approach throughout by stating clearly-defined objectives in each Step against which pupils' attainment can be measured as they engage in the teacher-directed activities. Links between the key objectives and STEPS are highlighted in the correlation guide so that teachers may more easily give emphasis to these in medium- and short-term planning.
12	**Parental involvement**	Parents are encouraged to help their children to become numerate.	Each Step includes ideas for involving parents or other family members through suggestions in the Home/School projects.

Issues for STEPS schools using the Framework to consider

- Although STEPS provides excellent coverage of most of the Framework's objectives, STEPS will have to be used in a different way.

- Teaching staff will need quick access to activities within STEPS (and, where appropriate, other teachers' resources) which support the learning objectives of the Framework. Each teacher will need ready access to more than one STEPS Handbook.

- Schools should consider and agree on how pupil materials are to be used.

- The Numeracy Strategy stresses the important part of homework in improving standards of numeracy.

- Storage of and access to STEPS materials should be reviewed.

- The Framework recommends a 'controlled degree of differentiated work on the topic being taught to the whole class'.

- STEPS Individual or Class Record Sheets will no longer be appropriate.

Notes on CM6: Issues for STEPS schools using the Framework to consider

■ **Although STEPS provides excellent coverage of most of the Framework's objectives, STEPS may have to be used in a different way.**

STEPS was designed to support the Programmes of Study for KS1 and KS2. The teaching activities in the STEPS Handbooks and the related pupils' materials have the following structure:

STEPS 1	for pupils working towards Level 1
STEPS 2	for pupils working towards Level 2
STEPS 3a and STEPS 3b	for pupils working towards Level 3
STEPS 4a and STEPS 4b	for pupils working towards Level 4
STEPS 5	for pupils working towards Level 5

The Yearly Teaching Programmes in the Framework have the following expectations:

Year 1	Level 1 and start on Level 2
Year 2	consolidation of Level 2 and start on Level 3
Year 3	revision of Level 2, but mainly Level 3
Year 4	consolidation of Level 3 and start on Level 4
Year 5	revision of Level 3, but mainly Level 4
Year 6	consolidation of Level 4 and start on Level 5

This means that for Year 1, for example, the activities which support the Framework will be found mainly in STEPS 1 and STEPS 2. This pattern repeats itself throughout Years 1 to 6, i.e. more than one Handbook will be needed to support the Framework's objectives for each year group.

STEPS Teacher's Handbooks

■ **Teaching staff will need quick access to activities within STEPS (and, where appropriate, other teachers' resources) which support the learning objectives of the Framework.**

In the STEPS Mathematics Correlation Guide to the Framework, objectives for each Yearly Teaching Programme (Reception to Year 6) are referenced to units within the STEPS Handbooks. Key objectives from the Framework are clearly distinguished from the other objectives.

Schools may also wish to reference sources of other teaching ideas to the objectives at the medium- or short-term planning stage.

■ **Each teacher will need ready access to more than one STEPS Handbook.**

The Handbooks need be used flexibly, e.g. by selecting only the activities which support the objectives from the Framework for the topic and which can be covered in the days allocated to the topic, and by using the Steps out of order. Whichever age group is being taught, each teacher will need access to more than one Handbook at different times.

Some schools using the Framework have chosen to rearrange the Steps in the Handbooks so that all the Steps relating to a particular topic in the Framework are collated in sequence. Where this approach is used, the contents pages at the front of each Handbook should be marked to indicate the topic to which each Step has been assigned. Where STEPS 1 and STEPS 2 are rearranged, users may wish to photocopy the final page of Steps units where the Steps finish on a right-hand page so that the units are complete (because the opening page of the next unit is on the reverse of that page).

Where gaps in STEPS coverage are identified, teaching ideas from other resources or drawn from the supplement of examples in the Framework will need to be planned.

Early years mathematics

The Early STEPS Teacher's Handbook continues to provide a teaching programme suitable for the early years.

STEPS Pupil materials

■ Schools should consider and agree on how pupil materials are to be used.

Even though STEPS is being used as the dominant resource, it is still advisable that pupils use other resources to fill gaps and to broaden their experience of ideas being presented in different ways.

Activity Books and Extra STEPS Activity Books (STEPS 1 and STEPS 2 only)

Pupils will not work through the Activity Books in order but will engage in activities selected by the teacher to support the learning objectives in the Framework.

Pupils will need access to more than one Activity Book (where used rather than the Activity Masters) within a short period of time. Schools may wish to allocate a full set of Activity Books to a child when written work is first considered appropriate and store them, e.g. in an envelope wallet for use at the discretion of the teacher.

The Extra STEPS Activity Books run in parallel with the Activity Books and can be used in the same way. Pages which are not selected for class work might be used for homework. (The Extra STEPS Activity Books are particularly suitable for this purpose.)

Activity Masters, Resource Masters and Differentiated Resource Masters

These can be photocopied selectively to support the learning objectives of particular lessons.

Pupil Books

Y2 pupils may need access to selected pages in the Textbooks accompanying STEPS 3a. If the Pupil Books are new to the children, some time may need to be allocated to familiarising the children with how to use them.

As with the Activity Books, pupils will not work through the Pupil Books in order but will engage in activities selected by the teacher to support the learning objectives in the Framework.

From Y3 onwards, pupils are likely to need access to different Pupil Books during the year (mainly two) so a storage system needs to be set up to make this possible.

Alternative pupils' resources may be needed in the few places where coverage in the STEPS Pupil Books is incomplete.

Homework

■ **The Numeracy Strategy stresses the important part of homework in improving standards of numeracy.**

Schools need to formalise a policy for homework so that it supports work in the classroom and to ensure an agreed approach throughout the school.

Ideas for Home/School Projects are included in each Step. For the early years in particular, selected projects could be chosen and typed up each term for parents to try out at home or a weekly notice could be displayed indicating how mathematics might be supported at home during that week.

In addition, schools might decide to send home Activity or Resource Masters which are not selected for or completed in classwork.

Extra STEPS Activity Books can also be used as an exclusive homework resource.

■ **Storage of and access to STEPS materials should be reviewed.**

Since teachers will need easy access to a variety of STEPS teacher and pupil resources for any of the Yearly Teaching Programmes, schools need to have an agreed system for storing, borrowing and replacing these.

In larger schools where more than one parallel class is covering a topic at the same time, it might be possible to have a flexible timetable, e.g. while one class is engaged in the literacy hour, the other is engaged in the numeracy hour, thus freeing more STEPS resources.

Differentiation

■ **The Framework recommends a 'controlled degree of differentiated work on the topic being taught to the whole class'.**

Schools need to agree a policy for catering for and monitoring the progress of the most- and least-able children and for those with special needs. A wide range of strategies should be considered. Some of these can be employed only when the need arises: others can be integrated into weekly plans. For example, you might like to consider:

• using or adapting the ideas in each Step for extending children who finish quickly, challenging the most able pupils and helping the least able;

• integrating selected Differentiated Resource Masters (from STEPS 3a onwards) into your weekly or daily planning sheets to cater for the top-, middle- and low-ability groups;

• asking open and closed questions which enable all children to participate in whole-class sessions;

• targeting time in each lesson so that at least one ability group can benefit from direct teaching focused on their particular needs, based on the same learning objectives wherever possible, but using objectives from the previous or following year, where appropriate;

• introducing some open-ended tasks linked to learning objectives which allow children to choose their own strategies, appropriate pace, method of recording and/or extension activities;

• setting with older children but aim to teach the same learning objectives to each set, perhaps varying the approach, pace and support appropriately, but acknowledging that even in a set class there is a range of ability and some targeted group work will still be necessary;

- make effective use of classroom helpers, e.g. NNEBs, parents etc. For example, your weekly plan might indicate when a helper is to work with a specific group and why;

- for the least able: simplifying text, providing apparatus (when other children may not need it), allowing extra time to consolidate an objective where the rest of the class move on to more demanding work;

- for the most able: providing more demanding tasks based on the objectives or selective 'dipping into' objectives from, for example, the following year's targets (but considering the problems the latter may cause for the teacher and children when they move to that year group).

- using the STEPS CD-ROM *The Maths Factory* which provides differentiated activities on a range of topics suitable for children in years Y3–Y6.

Record keeping

■ **STEPS Individual or Class Record Sheets will no longer be appropriate.**

The Framework states that 'it is not necessary or feasible to check and record each pupil's individual progress against every single teaching objective in mathematics'. However, it recommends that progress towards the key objectives should be recorded using, for example, a class record of key objectives.

Photocopiable Class Records Sheets to track progress against the key objectives are included for each year group R–Y6 in Section 5 on pp.62–69.

For the remaining objectives, the Framework states that children can be assumed to be living up to the expectations of your termly plan unless you indicate otherwise by keeping notes on children whose attainment is above or below this expectation. The next teacher can then assume that if notes are not passed over on a child, then that child is attaining in line with the Framework's expectations. (See pp.33–37 of 'Introducing the Framework'.)

YES, I'M SURE HE *IS* GOOD AT FETCHING YOUR DAD'S SLIPPERS, WAYNE, BUT HE'S NOT QUITE THE SORT OF CLASSROOM HELPER WE HAD IN MIND...

Medium- and short-term planning from the Framework

The Framework provides the basis for the long-term plan, and so from this you need to derive:

medium-term plans   termly or half-termly outlines of work and their main teaching objectives, and when you will teach them;

short-term plans   weekly or fortnightly notes on the tasks, activities, exercises, key questions and teaching points for five to ten mathematics lessons, including how pupils will be grouped and which of them you will work with.

This section includes procedures for medium- and short-term planning. They are presented merely as exemplars and can be modified to suit the particular requirements of a school. If possible, teachers should share the planning with at least one other colleague, e.g. a teacher with a parallel class.

Medium-term planning: Termly plan

Sample medium-term plans

A booklet of sample, completed medium-term plans for mathematics has been provided with the national training materials. These use the optional termly planning grids and are recommended as a 'starting point on which to build your own plans'.

Some schools may wish to use these initially to help with pace, coverage of the objectives and continuity, and to review and modify them as they are trialled. For these schools, the sheet for each year group R–Y6 in Section 4, 'Termly allocation of days to topics' might help.

Creating a school's own medium-term plans

The following procedure is appropriate for schools wishing to create their own planning grids. The Y2 objectives and optional termly planning templates have been used to demonstrate.

Creating a school's own medium-term plans

1. Use the Framework for reference.

2. Photocopy the Teaching Programme: Year 2 and Termly Planning Grid for each term.

3. Using the 'days' column on each Termly Planning Grid for guidance, allocate a provisional number of days for each topic specified within the row for each unit. (See pp.30–33 of this section.)

4. (Use of Section 4, 'Termly allocation of days to topics' might help.) Where several aspects are included within a topic, e.g. 'Measures and time, including problems', decide how many daily lessons should be allocated for each aspect, in this case, length, mass, capacity or time. Use column 5 for making any informal notes you find helpful. (See pp.30–33 of this section.)

5. Using a second copy of the termly planning grids, and teaching programme, write in the learning objectives for each week taking into account the number of days allocated to each topic. (See pp.34 and 35 of this section.)

In particular, make sure that key objectives are given emphasis. Try to make links between the objectives chosen so that numeracy lessons within a particular unit support each other. You could use highlighter pens to show what has been transferred to the templates.

6. Either termly or half-termly, repeat this procedure until templates for each term have been completed. Ensure that each objective for each topic is covered at least once in the year and that key objectives have been thoroughly covered.

7. Transfer these plans to short-term, e.g. fortnightly, weekly or daily, planning sheets. See pp.36–50 for short-term planning and sample lesson plans.

8. Collate your medium- and short-term plans with those of your colleagues to create a scheme of work for your school.

9. Trial, review and modify your termly plans using agreed monitoring criteria. (Modifying your plans is easiest if they are stored electronically.)

Sample completed termly planning sheet for the Autumn term of Year 2

Framework for teaching mathematics   Year 2: Autumn

Oral and mental: e.g. counting, mental strategies, rapid recall

Unit	Days	Pages	Topic	Notes
1	3	2-7	Counting and properties of numbers	*3 days*
2-4	15	8-19	Place value, ordering, estimating, rounding	*7 days*
		24-29	Understanding + and −	*3 days: Addition*
		32-41	Mental calculation strategies (+ and −)	*3 days: Subtraction*
		66-69	Money and 'real life' problems	
		58-61	Making decisions and checking results	*2 days: Link to addition/subtraction in context*
5-6	8	70-77	Measures, including problems	*3 days: Length (1)*
		80-89	Shape and space	*2 days: Capacity (1)*
		62-65	Reasoning about shapes	*3 days: 3-D shapes*
7	2		**Assess and review**	

Oral and mental: e.g. counting, mental strategies, rapid recall

Unit	Days	Pages	Topic	Notes
8	5	2-7	Counting and properties of numbers	*3 days*
		62-65	Reasoning about numbers	*2 days*
9	5	8-19	Place value, ordering, estimating, rounding	*2 days*
		24-29	Understanding + and −	*2 days: Mainly addition*
		32-41	Mental calculation strategies (+ and −)	
		66-69	Money and 'real life' problems	
		58-61	Making decisions and checking results	*1 day: Link to addition*
10-11	10	46-51	Understanding × and ÷	
		54-57	Mental calculation strategies (× and ÷)	*5 days: Emphasis on multiplication*
		66-69	Money and 'real life' problems	*2 days: Link to multiplication*
		58-61	Making decisions and checking results	*3 days: $\frac{1}{2}$ or $\frac{1}{4}$ of shapes*
		20-23	Fractions	
12-13	10	70-79	Measures, and time, including problems	*3 days: Time (1), order months*
				3 days: Mass (1)
		90-93	Handling data	*2 days: Graphs/pictograms (linked to time/mass)*
				2 days: Sorting diagrams
14	2		**Assess and review**	
Total	60			*my total = 56 days plus 4 days for review*

Note: Parts underlined show the emphasis for those days.

Sample completed termly planning sheet for the Spring term of Year 2

Framework for teaching mathematics   Year 2: Spring

Oral and mental: e.g. counting, mental strategies, rapid recall

Unit	Days	Pages	Topic	Notes
1	3	2-7	Counting and properties of numbers	*3 days*
2-4	15	8-19	Place value, ordering, estimating, rounding	*5 days*
		24-29	Understanding + and −	*5 days: Mainly subtraction*
		32-41	Mental calculation strategies (+ and −)	
		66-69	Money and 'real life' problems ⎫	*5 days: Money (1)*
		58-61	Making decisions and checking results ⎭	
5-6	8	70-77	Measures, including problems	*3 days: Length (2)*
		80-89	Shape and space ⎫	*2 days: Capacity (2)*
		62-65	Reasoning about shapes ⎭	*3 days: Position, direction, movement*
7	2		Assess and review	

Oral and mental: e.g. counting, mental strategies, rapid recall

Unit	Days	Pages	Topic	Notes
8	5	2-7	Counting and properties of numbers	*3 days*
		62-65	Reasoning about numbers	*2 days*
9	5	8-19	Place value, ordering, estimating, rounding	*2 days*
		24-29	Understanding + and −	*2 days: Mixed + and −*
		32-41	Mental calculation strategies (+ and −)	
		66-69	Money and 'real life' problems	
		58-61	Making decisions and checking results	*1 day: Link to + and − in context*
10	5	46-51	Understanding × and ÷	*2 days: Emphasis on ÷ (halving)*
		54-57	Mental calculation strategies (× and ÷)	
		66-69	Money and 'real life' problems ⎫	*1 day: Link to division*
		58-61	Making decisions and checking results ⎭	
		20-23	Fractions	*2 days: ½ or ¼ of quantities*
11-12	10	70-79	Measures, and time, including problems	*3 days: Time (2)* *3 days: Mass (1)*
		90-93	Handling data	*2 days: Emphasis on tables/lists* *2 days: Sorting diagrams*
13	2		**Assess and review**	
Total	55			*my total = 51 days plus 4 days for review*

Sample completed termly planning sheet for the Summer term of Year 2

Framework for teaching mathematics   Year 2: Summer

Oral and mental: e.g. counting, mental strategies, rapid recall

Unit	Days	Pages	Topic	Notes
1	3	2-7	Counting and properties of numbers	*3 days*
2-4	15	8-19	Place value, ordering, estimating, rounding	*5 days*
		24-29	Understanding + and −	*3 days: Emphasis on addition*
		32-41	Mental calculation strategies (+ and −)	*3 days: Emphasis on subtraction*
		66-69	Money and 'real life' problems	*4 days: Money (2) Link to addition/subtraction*
		58-61	Making decisions and checking results	
5-6	8	70-77	Measures, including problems	*2 days: Length (3)*
		80-89	Shape and space	*2 days: Capacity (3)*
		62-65	Reasoning about shapes	*4 days: Emphasis on 2-D shapes*
7	2		**Assess and review**	

Oral and mental: e.g. counting, mental strategies, rapid recall

Unit	Days	Pages	Topic	Notes
8	5	2-7	Counting and properties of numbers	*3 days*
		62-65	Reasoning about numbers	*2 days*
9	5	8-19	Place value, ordering, estimating, rounding	*2 days*
		24-29	Understanding + and −	
		32-41	Mental calculation strategies (+ and −)	*2 days: Emphasis on addition*
		66-69	Money and 'real life' problems	*1 day: Number stories for 'sums'*
		58-61	Making decisions and checking results	
10-11	10	46-51	Understanding × and ÷	*5 days: Emphasis on division, halving as inverse of doubling*
		54-57	Mental calculation strategies (× and ÷)	
		66-69	Money and 'real life' problems	*2 days: Link to ÷ problems*
		58-61	Making decisions and checking results	
		20-23	Fractions	*3 days*
12-13	10	70-79	Measures, and time, including problems	*3 days: Time (3)* *3 days: Mass (3)*
		90-93	Handling data	*4 days: Emphasis on block graphs/pictograms*
14	2		Assess and review	
Total	60			*my total = 56 days plus 4 days for review*

Sample of Autumn coverage chosen from Yearly Teaching Programme for Year 2

Key objectives are highlighted in **bold type**.

Page references are to the supplement of examples for Years 1, 2 and 3.

The objectives which are underlined have been transferred to the Y2 planning grid for the Autumn term (see pages 36–37).

The selected objectives from the Yearly Teaching Programme for the Autumn term for Year 2 (pages 33 and 35) have been underlined since it is not possible to highlight them in colour in this book. However, for schools engaging in this planning process, the use of highlighter pens is recommended, e.g.

Autumn term: blue highlight
Spring term: yellow highlight
Summer term: pink highlight

When an objective for the Autumn term is covered again in a different term, additional colours of highlighter can overlay the blue one. For example, if blue and yellow highlighted lines are drawn over an objective, the resultant green highlighter will indicate coverage in two consecutive terms.

Where parts of an objective are not covered, the underlining is not used, e.g. the standard unit of measurement 'cm' has not yet been covered in the length topic in the Measures strand.

Numbers and the number system

2-7	**Counting, properties of numbers and number sequences**
3	Say the number names in order to at least 100, from and back to zero
3	Count reliably up to 100 objects by grouping them: for example, in tens, then in fives or twos
3, 5, 7	**Describe and extend simple number sequences: count on or back in ones or tens, starting from any two-digit number;** count in hundreds from and back to zero; count on in twos from and back to zero or any small number, **and recognise odd and even numbers** to at least 30; count on in steps of 3, 4 or 5 to at least 30, from and back to zero, then from and back to any given small number
7	Begin to recognise two-digit multiples of 2, 5 or 10
8-15	**Place value and ordering**
9	**Read and write whole numbers to at least 100 in figures and words**
9	**Know what each digit in a two-digit number represents, including 0 as a place holder, and partition two-digit numbers into a multiple of ten and ones (TU)**
11	Use and begin to read the vocabulary of comparing and ordering numbers, including ordinal numbers to 100 Use the = sign to represent equality Compare two given two-digit numbers, say which is more or less, and give a number which lies between them
13	Say the number that is 1 or 10 more or less than any given two-digit number
15	**Order whole numbers to at least 100,** and position them on a number line and 100 square
16-19	**Estimating and rounding**
17	Use and begin to read the vocabulary of estimation and approximation; give a sensible estimate of at least 50 objects
19	Round numbers less than 100 to the nearest 10
20-23	**Fractions**
21, 23	Begin to recognise and find one half and one quarter of shapes and small numbers of objects Begin to recognise that two halves or four quarters make one whole and that two quarters and one half are equivalent

Calculations

24-29 Understanding addition and subtraction

25, 29 Extend understanding of the operations of addition and subtraction

Use and begin to read the related vocabulary

Use the +, − and = signs to record mental additions and subtractions in a number sentence, and recognise the use of a symbol such as □ or △ to stand for an unknown number

Recognise that addition can be done in any order, but not subtraction: for example, 3 + 21 = 21 + 3, but 21 − 3 ≠ 3 − 21

27 Understand that more than two numbers can be added

Begin to add three single-digit numbers mentally (totals up to about 20) or three two-digit numbers with the help of apparatus (totals up to 100)

25, 29 **Understand that subtraction is the inverse of addition** (subtraction reverses addition)

30-31 Rapid recall of addition and subtraction facts

31 **Know by heart:**

all addition and subtraction facts for each number to at least 10;

all pairs of numbers with a total of 20 (e.g. 13 + 7, 6 + 14);

all pairs of multiples of 10 with a total of 100 (e.g. 30 + 70)

32-41 Mental calculation strategies (+ and −)

33 **Use knowledge that addition can be done in any order to do mental calculations more efficiently.**
For example:

put the larger number first and count on in tens or ones;

add three small numbers by putting the largest number first and/or find a pair totalling 10;

partition into '5 and a bit' when adding 6, 7, 8 or 9, then recombine (e.g. 16 + 8 = 15 + 1 + 5 + 3 = 20 + 4 = 24);

partition additions into tens and units, then recombine

33 Find a small difference by counting up from the smaller to the larger number (e.g. 42 − 39)

33 Identify near doubles, using doubles already known (e.g. 8 + 9, 40 + 41)

35 Add/subtract 9 or 11: add/subtract 10 and adjust by 1
Begin to add/subtract 19 or 21: add/ subtract 20 and adjust by 1

35 Use patterns of similar calculations

35 **State the subtraction corresponding to a given addition, and vice versa**

37, 39 Use known number facts and place value to add/subtract mentally

41 Bridge through 10 or 20, then adjust

46-51 Understanding multiplication and division

47, 49 Understand the operation of multiplication as repeated addition or as describing an array, and begin to understand division as grouping (repeated subtraction) or sharing

Use and begin to read the related vocabulary

Use the ×, ÷ and = signs to record mental calculations in a number sentence, and recognise the use of a symbol such as □ or △ to stand for an unknown number

47, 49 **Know and use halving as the inverse of doubling**

52-53 Rapid recall of multiplication and division facts

53 **Know by heart:**

multiplication facts for the 2 and 10 times-tables;

doubles of all numbers to 10 and the corresponding halves

Begin to know:

multiplication facts for the 5 times-table

53 Derive quickly:

division facts corresponding to the 2 and 10 times-tables;

doubles of all numbers to at least 15 (e.g. 11 + 11 or 11 × 2);

doubles of multiples of 5 to 50 (e.g. 20 × 2 or 35 × 2);

halves of multiples of 10 to 100 (e.g. half of 70)

54-57 Mental calculation strategies × and ÷

57 Use known number facts and place value to carry out mentally simple multiplications and divisions

58-59 Checking results of calculations

59 Repeat addition in a different order

59 Check with an equivalent calculation

Solving problems

60-61 Making decisions

61 **Choose and use appropriate operations and efficient calculation strategies** (e.g. mental, mental with jottings) **to solve problems**

62-65 Reasoning about numbers or shapes

63 Solve mathematical problems or puzzles, recognise simple patterns and relationships, generalise and predict. Suggest extensions by asking 'What if...?' or 'What could I try next?'

65 Investigate a general statement about familiar numbers or shapes by finding examples that satisfy it

65 **Explain how a problem was solved** orally, and where appropriate, in writing

66-71 Problems involving 'real life', money or measures

67, 69, 71 Use mental addition and subtraction, simple multiplication and division, to solve simple word problems involving numbers in 'real life', money or measures, using one or two steps. Explain how the problem was solved.

69 Recognise all coins and begin to use £.p notation for money (for example, know that £4.65 indicates £4 and 65p)
Find totals, give change, and work out which coins to pay

90-93 Organising and using data

91, 93 Solve a given problem by sorting, classifying and organising information in simple ways, such as:
in a list or simple table;
in a pictogram;
in a block graph
Discuss and explain results

Measures, shape and space

72-79 Measures

73 Use and begin to read the vocabulary related to length, mass and capacity

73, 75 **Estimate, measure and compare lengths, masses and capacities, using standard units (m, cm, kg, litre); suggest suitable units and equipment for such measurements**

77 **Read a simple scale to the nearest labelled division, including using a ruler to draw and measure lines to the nearest centimetre**, recording estimates and measurements as '3 and a bit metres long' or 'about 8 centimetres' or 'nearly 3 kilograms heavy'

79 Use and begin to read the vocabulary related to time
Use units of time and know the relationships between them (second, minute, hour, day, week)
Suggest suitable units to estimate or measure time
Order the months of the year
Read the time to the hour, half hour or quarter hour on an analogue clock and a 12-hour digital clock, and understand the notation 7:30

80-89 Shape and space

81 **Use the mathematical names for common 3-D and 2-D shapes**, including the pyramid, cylinder, pentagon, hexagon, octagon...

81 **Sort shapes and describe some of their features**, such as the number of sides and corners, symmetry (2-D shapes), or the shapes of faces and number of faces, edges and corners (3-D shapes).

83 Make and describe shapes, pictures and patterns, using for example, solid shapes, templates, pinboard and elastic bands, squared paper, a programmable robot...
Relate solid shapes to pictures of them

85 Begin to recognise line symmetry

87, 89 **Use mathematical vocabulary to describe position, direction and movement**: for example, describe, place, tick, draw or visualise objects in given positions

87, 89 Recognise whole, half and quarter turns, to the left or right, clockwise or anti-clockwise
Know that a right angle is a measure of a quarter turn, and recognise right angles in squares and rectangles
Give instructions for moving along a route in straight lines and round right-angled corners: for example, to pass through a simple maze...

Sample termly plan

The objectives on this plan are taken from the Yearly Teaching Programme: Y2.

Key objectives are shown in bold text.

The page references refer to the supplement of examples in the Framework and should inform your choice of activities when daily lessons are planned in detail.

Oral and mental skills: These should be practised daily for 5–10 minutes. They may or may not be linked to the main teaching activity. On the planning grid below, the page numbers in this section refer to the pages of exemplars; the number in brackets indicates the number of days provisionally allocated to that objective. These are blocked to correspond with the number of days in the units in the main part of the planning grid, i.e. 3, 15 and 8 days for the three units in the first half of the Autumn term.

Year 2: Autumn ~~and Summer~~

Oral and mental skills: e.g. counting, mental strategies, rapid recall

p.3 Say the number names in order to at least 100 (3)
p.31 **Know by heart: addition facts for each number to at least 10** (5)
p.31 **Know by heart: subtraction facts for each number to at least 10** (5)
p.13 Say the number which is one or 10 more/less than any given two-digit number (5)
p.33 Add three small numbers by putting the largest number first and/or find a pair totalling 10 (4)
p.53 Derive quickly doubles of all numbers to 10 and corresponding halves (4)

Unit	Days	Pages	Topic	Objectives: children will be taught to
1	3	2-7	Counting and properties of numbers	Say the number names in order to at least 100, from and back to zero.
2-4	5	8-19	Place value, ordering, estimating, rounding	**Read and write whole numbers to at least 100 in figures and words**
	8	24-29	Understanding + and −	Addition: Extend understanding of the operations of addition; use + and = signs to record mental additions in a number sentence and recognise the use of a symbol such as □ or △ to stand for an unknown number. Subtraction: Extend understanding of the operations of subtraction; use − and = signs to record mental subtractions in a number sentence and recognise the use of a symbol such as □ or △ to stand for an unknown number. Strategy: Put the larger number first in order to count on.
		32-41	Mental calculation strategies (+ and −)	
	2	66-69	Money and 'real life' problems	Addition and subtraction: Solve simple problems in 'real-life' contexts and explain how the problem was solved. Check results: Repeat addition in a different order (check results).
		58-61	Making decisions and checking results	
	~~15~~			
5-6	3	70-77	Measures, including problems	Length: Use and begin to read the vocabulary related to length; **Estimate, measure and compare lengths using metres.**
	2			Capacity: Use and begin to read the vocabulary related to capacity; **Estimate, measure and compare capacity using litres.**
	3	80-89	Shape and space Reasoning about shapes	3-D shapes: **Use the mathematical names for common 3-D shapes** including the pyramid and cylinder. **Sort shapes and describe some of their features** such as the shapes of the faces or the number of faces, edges and corners.
	~~8~~			
7	2		**Assess and review**	

Year 2: Autumn and Summer (continued)

Oral and mental skills: e.g. counting, mental strategies, rapid recall

p.3 **Count on or back in tens starting from any two-digit number** (3)
p.31 Revision: **know by heart all addition and subtraction facts for each number to 10** (2)
p.31 Recall of all pairs of numbers with a total of 20 (5)
p.53 Rapid recall of multiplication facts for the 10 times-table (5)
p.31 Recall of all pairs of multiples of 10 with a total of 100 (5)
p.53 Revision: Derive quickly doubles of all numbers to 20 and corresponding halves (4)
p.5 Revision: **Count on or back in ones or tens starting from any two-digit number** (2)
p.35 Add or subtract 9 to two-digit numbers – add/subtract 10 and adjust by 1 (4)

Unit	Days	Pages	Topic	Objectives: children will be taught to
8	3	2-7	Counting and properties of numbers	Count reliably up to 100 objects by grouping them in tens. Describe and extend simple number sequences: count on or back in ones or tens.
	2	62-65	Reasoning about numbers	Solve puzzles and problems: How many dominoes have an odd (even) number of spots? Sort dominoes in different ways.
	5			
9	2	8-19	Place value, ordering, estimating, rounding	**Know what each digit in a two-digit number represents, including 0 as a place-holder.** Partition two-digit numbers into tens and ones.
	2	24-29	Understanding + and −	Addition: Respond rapidly to oral/written questions phrased in a variety of ways. Strategy: Add three small numbers by putting the largest number first and/or find a pair totalling 10.
	1	32-41	Mental calculation strategies (+ and −)	
		66-69	Money and 'real life' problems	Solve 'story' problems which use addition.
		58-61	Making decisions and checking results	**Choose and use appropriate operations and efficient calculation strategies** (by explaining and recording how the problem was solved).
	5			
10-11	5	46-51	Understanding × and ÷	**Understand the operation of multiplication as repeated subtraction or as describing an array.** Use and begin to read the related vocabulary. Strategy: Use known number facts and place value to carry out mentally simple multiplications.
		54-57	Mental calculation strategies × and ÷	
	2	66-69	Money and 'real life' problems	Use simple multiplication to solve simple word problems involving numbers in 'real-life' using one or two steps. **Choose and use appropriate operations and efficient calculation strategies** (by explaining and recording how the problem was solved).
		58-61	Making decisions and checking results	
	3	20-23	Fractions	Begin to recognise and find one half and one quarter of shapes.
	10			
12-13	3	70-79	Measures, and time, including problems	Time: Use and begin to read the vocabulary related to time. Order the months of the year. Mass: **Estimate, measure and compare masses using standard units (kg).**
	4	90-93	Handling data	Solve a given problem by sorting, classifying and organising information: in a pictogram; in a block graph.
	10			
14	2		**Assess and review**	
Total	60			

Short-term planning: Weekly plan

Unit 9 of the Spring Term for Y2 has been chosen to demonstrate a short-term (weekly) plan for this 5-day unit.

---

1. Refer to the completed Termly Planning Template for Y2 Autumn Term, the Framework's supplement of examples and the STEPS Mathematics Correlation to the Framework.

2. Transfer the objectives for Unit 9 to a weekly lesson plan (whose design has previously been agreed with all the staff and which takes into account the recommendations of the Framework for a typical daily lesson).

Please note: Since the units do not fall neatly into weekly or fortnightly blocks of time, some schools may prefer to prepare short-term plans for units (which range from 3 to 15 days). Unit numbers approximate to the number of weeks in a term.

3. Find the cross-reference to the Framework topics/objectives in Section 6, 'Correlation to the National Framework'.

4. Using the supplement of examples in the Framework to inform your choice, select suitable activities from the appropriate Steps and other resources which cover the learning objectives. See CM8 (pp.40–41) for a sample completed weekly lesson plan and CM9 (pp.42–43) for a template of this plan.

Short-term planning: Daily plan

Alternatively, select a suitable activity to enter on a daily lesson plan. See CM10 (p.44) for a sample completed daily lesson plan for Day 1 of Unit 12/13 for the Summer Term: Y2, and CM11 (p.45) for a template of this plan.

Coordinator's notes
CM7(p.39) explains briefly the headings on CM8 (Weekly plan) and CM10 (Daily plan).

Weekly and daily plans: headings used

Oral/mental work

5–10 minute starter with whole class – emphasis on counting, mental strategies, number facts, quick recall, etc.

Main activity

Objectives from the Framework

Objective(s) or selected part of objective(s) taken from the Framework.

Key vocabulary

Taken from supplement of examples in the Framework and/or Key Vocabulary box in STEPS Handbooks.

Key idea

Can indicate which particular part of an objective is the main focus for a particular day if one objective is the focus for several days.

May be taken from the Framework's supplement of examples for each year group.

May be an open-ended question to which all the class can respond.

Resources

STEPS materials or other resources (including apparatus) which support the lesson plan.

Main activity

How to introduce and develop the main activity with the whole class.

Differentiated tasks

How you intend to cater for the range of ability:

1 high ability;
2 middle ability (who may be seated at two or more tables);
3 low ability.

Groups targeted for direct teaching are boxed on the sample completed plans.

Plenary

How you intend to round off the lesson.
This may need to be changed to respond to what happens in the lesson.

Evaluation

Any notes which will inform future lessons.

Y2 Weekly Plan: Daily Mathematics Lessons

	Monday	Tuesday
Oral/mental work	**Count on in ones or tens, starting from any two-digit number**	**Count on in ones or tens starting from any two-digit number**
Main activity objectives from Framework	**Know what each digit in a two-digit number represents, including the use of zero as a place-holder**	Partition two-digit numbers into a multiple of ten and ones.
Key vocabulary	tens, ones, units, number names, e.g. sixty-three, smallest/largest number, one/two-digit number	As for Monday
Key idea	Model two-digit numbers using rods of tens and units.	Consolidation of Monday's activity – recording: 40 + 6 = 46
Resources	STEPS 2:24 C – resources as stated	STEPS 2:24 C, Activity Book 2: 24, pp 21-22
Main activity	Introduction: Lesson plan 2:24 C, stages 1 and 2. Development: Follow lesson plan stages 3 to 6.	Introduction: What did you learn yesterday? Development: Introduce activities in the Activity Books.
Differentiated tasks (where appropriate)	Group 1 Group 2 Group 3 Adapt for multiples of 10 only if necessary	Group 1 How many different two-digit numbers using 2, 3, 6 and 9? Group 2 Activity Book Group 3 Activity Book: support teacher
Plenary	Develop stage 7 of 2:24 C (use of zero as a place holder).	Demonstration: children writing numbers in the form 65 = 60 + 5.
Evaluation		

Note: **Key objectives** are shown in bold.

Wednesday	Thursday	Friday
Count back in ones or tens starting from any two-digit number	Count back in ones or tens starting from any two-digit number	Count on or back in ones or tens starting from any two-digit number
Understand the operation of addition and the related vocabulary	Know by heart all pairs of multiples of ten with totals to 100 (revision)	**Choose and use appropriate operations and efficient calculation strategies.**
Flash cards displayed: more, add, sum, total, plus, altogether, equals, +, −, displayed	As for Wednesday, also multiple	Flashcards displayed as for Wednesday
Respond rapidly to oral questions phrased in a variety of ways/linking spoken and written forms using flash cards.	Applying knowledge of adding pairs of multiples of 10.	Making up number stories to reflect statements such as '15 + 3' (totals to 20).
Digit cards 0-9 for each child. Use STEPS 1: Resource Master 6).	STEPS 3A: 7 B. Base 10 longs	Framework, p 61
Introduction: Explain – Hold up your digit cards to show answers to my addition problems. Development: Show me the total of 27 and 10; the sum of 5 and 15; two numbers which total 14; what must I add to 8 to make 17, etc.	Introduction: Explain objectives of lesson. Development: Follow lesson plan.	Introduction: Children suggest 'stories' for 15 + 3 = 18, written as sentences on board – use range of vocabulary. Development: Write five further additions on board.
Group 1 Recording addition 'word' sentences with totals greater than 20. Group 2 As for the group 1 but with extra support. Group 3 Recording addition sentences with totals greater than 10 using +, =.	Group 1 Resource Master 25 Group 2 Resource Master 25 Group 3 Allow access to base 10 longs/support teacher	Group 1 Paired work: group generate own sentences using totals beyond 20 Group 2 Individuals generate sentences for five displayed additions then create own. Group 3 As for 2 but allow access to number lines throughout.
Display: The total of 5 and □ is ☆ – children offer solutions and read sentences to class.	Discussion: Display: 100 = ○ + ○ + ○ (multiples of 10 to be inserted) – children suggest solutions.	Tell number stories – children demonstrate how to write these as a sum using = and +.

Y__ Weekly Plan: Daily Mathematics Lessons

	Monday	Tuesday
Oral/mental work		
Main activity objectives from Framework		
Key vocabulary		
Key idea		
Resources		
Main activity	Introduction: Development:	Introduction: Development:
Differentiated tasks (where appropriate)	Group 1 Group 2 Group 3	Group 1 Group 2 Group 3
Plenary		
Evaluation		

Class: Term: Unit: Week:

Wednesday	Thursday	Friday
Introduction: Development:	Introduction: Development:	Introduction: Development:
Group 1 Group 2 Group 3	Group 1 Group 2 Group 3	Group 1 Group 2 Group 3

Daily Plan

Year: 2   **Term**: Summer

Topic: Time   **Week**: 12   **Day**: 1   **Unit**: 12/13   **Framework**: p.79

Oral/mental work

Derive quickly halves of multiples of 10 to 100.

Main activity
objectives from Framework

a) Use and begin to read the vocabulary related to time;
b) Order the months of the year.

Key vocabulary

month, year, next, before, after, between, 1st to 12th

Key idea

Order the months of the year

Resources

Teacher   STEPS 2:25 E

Pupils   Resource Master 71

Main activity

Introduction   Q: What is your favourite month? Why?

Development   Follow lesson plan in STEPS 2:25 E

Differentiated tasks

Group 1 Resource Master 71

Group 2 Resource Master 71

Group 3 Support teacher – assist with reading problems – Resource Master 71

Plenary

Teacher and children give clues for others to guess the month,
e.g. Name the month between May and July; name all the months beginning with J.

Evaluation

Daily Plan

Year: **Term:**

Topic: **Week:**   **Day:**   **Unit:**   **Framework:**

Oral/mental work

Main activity
objectives from Framework

Key vocabulary

Key idea

Resources
    Teacher
    Pupils

Main activity
    Introduction

    Development

Differentiated tasks
    Group 1

    Group 2

    Group 3

Plenary

Evaluation

Sample lesson plans

The final part of this section offers examples of individual daily maths lessons plans with STEPS. The lesson plans show how one topic – in this case Fractions – could be treated during the three terms of Year 2. Having worked through the termly and weekly planning, this teacher has allotted a total of 4 daily lessons to the topic.

All the objectives for the Fractions topic in the Y2 Yearly Teaching Programme are covered and the topic is revisited at least once each term.

Summary

Year: 2

Topic: Fractions

Objectives: (Taken from the Framework for Teaching Mathematics)

Begin to recognise and find one half and one quarter of shapes and small numbers of objects.

Begin to recognise that two halves or four quarters make one whole and that two quarters and one half are equivalent.

Time allocation:

Autumn term	1 day
Spring term	2 days
Summer term	1 day
Total	4 days

These lesson plans are included as examples of how daily lessons can be organised using STEPS. The final plan (CM14) shows how the same planning template can be adapted for the few instances where there is a gap in STEPS coverage. Once you have identified which topics will be covered in a particular week, the correlation chart at the end of this Handbook enables you to find the STEPS reference which covers the relevant objective. You will then be able to follow tor adapt the lesson plan for that STEP.

In the part of the plan headed 'Main activity', the teacher has indicated which groups are to be targeted for additional teacher support and in what order. For example, on the first plan, 10–15 minutes will be spent with Target Group 1 before Target Group 2 has its turn.

Fractions Year 2: Autumn term (1 day)

Oral and mental starter	All pairs of numbers with a total of 20
	Framework page 31: Children say how many more counters are needed to make 20, and explain strategy
Learning objectives	Begin to recognise and name one half of shapes
Time allocation	Autumn term: week 11, day 5
STEPS reference	STEPS 2:34 Activity B

Resources	**Vocabulary**
as for STEPS 2:34 B	half, halve, halving, halves, exactly, equal, fraction, divide

Introduction

Explain to the children that they are going to learn about halves.
Ask children to describe/demonstrate what they think is meant by a half.
Provide each group with a supply of gummed paper shapes.
Follow stages 1 and 2 of Steps 2:34B.
Repeat stages 1 and 2 for an isosceles triangle.

Main activity (whole class)

1. Preparing own display of other halved shapes.
2. Target Group 2: Children prepare their own display of other halved shapes.
   Teacher reinforces language and why the shapes show halves.
3. Target Group 1: Children observe extra teacher demonstrations.
   Children prepare their own display of other halved shapes.

Plenary

Children discuss/demonstrate which shapes could be folded in half in one than one way.

Fractions Year 2: Spring term (2 days)

Oral and mental starter	State the subtraction corresponding to a given addition and vice versa Framework page 35: Children write and say aloud addition/subtractions made from trios such as 8, 9, 17
Learning objectives	Begin to recognise and name one quarter of shapes
Time allocation	Spring term: week 10, day 4
STEPS reference	Steps 3a:23 Activity G

Resources
as for Steps 2:34 G
1cm squared grid

Vocabulary
half, halve, halves, quarter, exactly, equal parts, fraction, divide

Introduction
Recap: Children discuss/demonstrate what they remember about halves.
Ask: How can you find half of a square?
Explain to the children that they are going to learn about quarters.
Provide each group with a supply of gummed paper shapes.
Follow stages 1 and 2 of Steps 2:34B but adapt for quarters as suggested in 2:34G.

Main activity (3 groups)
1. Target Goup 1: Teacher demonstrates/discusses how different rectangles can be drawn on squared grid and quarters shown. Children draw different rectangles and divide them into quarters.
2. Children prepare their own display of shapes divided into quarters; Activity Master 2:64.
3. Support teacher:
   Same as Group 2 but supervised
   Emphasis on spoken language and discussion of examples of quarters
   Activity Master 2:64

Plenary
Draw several shapes on the board, all divided into four parts but not always showing quarters. Discuss which show quarters and why. Children add to board display.

Fractions Year 2: Spring term (2 days)

Oral and mental starter	State the subtraction corresponding to a given addition and vice versa
	Framework page 35: Teacher says aloud an addition (totals to 20) e.g. 4 + 7 = 11; children take turns to say to partner the corresponding subtraction, then check with teacher
Learning objectives	Begin to recognise and name one half and one quarter of shapes
Time allocation	Spring term: week 10, day 5
STEPS reference	Steps 3a:23 Activity E

Resources
as for STEPS 2:34 B

Vocabulary
half, halve, halving, halves, quarter, exactly, share equally, fraction, divide, set

Introduction
Recap: Children discuss/demonstrate what they remember about quarters.
Ask: How can you find one quarter of a square? How many ways can you show?
Explain that today they will learn to find halves and quarters of numbers of objects.
Provide each child with 20 interlocking cubes.
Follow stage 1 Steps 2:34I but adapt so that children find halves and quarters.

Main activity (whole class)
1. Target Group 2: Activity Master 2:65 (or Activity Book 2c, page 9). Teacher discusses examples on activity sheet – on completion, ask children to create own examples to show half and quarter of a set.
2. Target Group 1: Reinforce language and strategies for finding halves and quarters; introduce Activity Master 65; make up more examples if finished early.
3. Making rods in two colours to show halves; then four colours to show quarters as in Activities 2:34 K and L.

Plenary
Use Group 3's rods for discussion. Encourage children to suggest numbers to go in these sentences:

$\frac{1}{2}$ of $\square$ cubes = $\square$ cubes   and $\frac{1}{4}$ of $\square$ cubes = $\square$ cubes

Fractions Year 2: Summer term (1 day)

Learning objectives	Begin to recognise that two halves or four quarters make one whole and that two quarters and one half are equivalent
Time allocation	Summer term: week 11, day 5
STEPS reference	New activity

Resources

Gummed squares, circles or regular hexagons, one for each pair of children
Each pair of children need:
- six 10 cm squares of paper
- dice or spinner marked $\frac{1}{2}$, $\frac{1}{2}$, $\frac{1}{4}$, $\frac{1}{4}$, $\frac{1}{4}$, $\frac{1}{4}$
- scissors

Vocabulary

half, halve, halving, halves, quarter, exact, equal, fraction , share, whole, equivalent, same

Introduction

Give pairs of children one shape to share.
Ask them to fold their shape to show halves.
Ask: How many halves make a whole? What is special about two halves?
Now ask them to fold their paper again to show quarters.
Ask: How many quarters make a whole? What is special about four quarters?

Main activity – whole class game

Give pairs of children six paper squares to share.
Explain the game. They will need to:
- leave two squares uncut and write '1 whole' on them
- cut two in half and write '1 half' on each piece
- cut two into quarters and write '1 quarter' on each piece.

Players begin with a whole square each then take turns to:
- roll the dice
- take the appropriate fraction and place it on their 'whole'.

They miss a turn if there isn't space to fit the fraction they roll on their 'whole'.
The first player to cover their 'whole' scores one point.
Repeat the game until one player scores three points to win.

Plenary

Ask: What fractions could you use to cover the whole shape?
Display the selections. Draw attention to the following:
- that two quarters fill the same space as a half
- four quarters are equivalent to a whole
- two halves are equivalent to a whole.

Termly allocation of days to topic (R–Y6)

CMs 15 to 21 give a suggested breakdown of the number of days it is reasonable to allocate to the topics within the Framework. Schools may need to adjust these to suit their particular needs.

The Copymasters will be useful to refer to at the medium-term planning stage, whether or not the termly planning templates are being used, to:

■ compare arrangements which exist in a school with those required by the Framework;

■ indicate the increasing or decreasing significance of different topics as children move up through the year groups;

■ ensure that the topics are taught in a balanced way.

The order in which the topics are presented to the children can be varied. This might be particularly important in schools where resources are not plentiful so that, say, the resources for length are not needed by more than one teacher at the same time.

When planning without the templates, try to link related topics together to avoid 'atomising' teaching and learning. For example, some of the days allocated to the topics, 'Understanding addition/subtraction', 'Rapid recall of addition and subtraction facts' and 'Mental calculation strategies' can run consecutively to maximise patterns and relationships within addition and subtraction.

It will not always be possible to plan so that the allocation of days for a topic ends on a Friday.

Allocation of days to topic: YR

Topic	Number of days		
	Autumn	Spring	Summer
Numbers and the number system			
Counting	18	7	7
Reading and writing numbers	0	5	6 †
Comparing and ordering numbers	3	5	4
Calculations			
Adding and subtracting	5	8	9
Solving problems			
Reasoning about numbers or shapes	2	3	2
Problems involving real life or money	2	2	2
Measures, shape and space			
Comparing and ordering measures	6	7	6
Exploring pattern, shape and space	8	7	8
Assess and review	4	4	4
Total (days each term)	**48**	**48**	**48** ‡

† Not required by the objectives for the Autumn term but can be integrated informally into lessons on counting, where appropriate, provided the emphasis is on counting skills.

‡ A nominal 44 daily lessons and 4 days for the assess/review has/have been allocated to each term but this may have to be varied to suit the circumstances within a school, e.g. time needed for children to settle into school.

For children who spend a full year in Reception, aim to cover the objectives in the Yearly Teaching Programme. For all children, particular emphasis should be given in planning so that at most children succeed with the key objectives.

Allocation of days to topic: Y1

Topic	Number of days		
	Autumn	**Spring**	**Summer**
Numbers and the number system			
Counting/properties of numbers/sequences	6	6	6
Place value and ordering	8	7	8
Estimating	2	1	2
Calculations			
Understanding addition/subtraction	6	6	6
Rapid recall of addition and subtraction facts	0	0	0 †
Mental calculation strategies + / −	4	3	4
Solving problems			
Making decisions	3	3	3
Reasoning about numbers or shapes	3	3	3
Problems involving real life, money or measures	7	6	7
Organising and using data	5	5	5
Measures, shape and space			
Measures	8	9	8
Shape and space	4	2	4
Assess and review	4	4	4
Total (days each term)	60	55	60

Number of days allocated to different topics has been kept comparable as far as possible to assist with whole-class planning.

† To be practised daily.

Allocation of days to topic: Y2

Topic	Number of days		
	Autumn	Spring	Summer
Numbers and the number system			
Counting/properties of numbers/sequences	6	6	6
Place value and ordering	4	4	4
Estimating and rounding	2	2	2
Fractions	3	1	3
Calculations			
Understanding addition/subtraction	4	4	4
Rapid recall of addition and subtraction facts	0	0	0 †
Mental calculation strategies + / −	3	3	3
Understanding multiplication/division	3	1	3
Rapid recall of multiplication/division facts	0	0	0 †
Mental calculation strategies × / ÷	1	1	1
Checking results of calculations	4	4	4 ‡
Solving problems			
Making decisions	0	0	0 ‡
Reasoning about numbers or shapes	3	3	3
Problems involving real life, money or measures	6	6	6
Organising and using data	5	5	5
Measures, shape and space			
Measures	8	9	8
Shape and space	4	2	4
Assess and review	4	4	4
Total (days each term)	60	55	60

To assist mixed Y1/Y2 classes, the number of days allocated to different topics has been kept comparable as far as possible to assist with whole-class planning.

† To be practised daily.

‡ 9 days in total allocated to 'making decisions and checking results'.

Allocation of days to topic: Y3

Topic	Number of days		
	Autumn	Spring	Summer
Numbers and the number system			
Counting/properties or numbers/sequences	3	3	3
Place value and ordering	1	2	1
Estimating and rounding	1	0	1
Fractions	5	5	5
Calculations			
Understanding addition/subtraction	4	5	2
Rapid recall of addition and subtraction facts	0	0	0 †
Mental calculation strategies + / −	3	3	1
Pencil and paper procedures + / −	0	0	4
Understanding multiplication/division	3	3	3
Rapid recall of multiplication/division facts	0	0	0 †
Mental calculation strategies × / ÷	2	1	2
Checking results of calculations	6	3	6 ‡
Solving problems			
Making decisions	0	0	0 ‡
Reasoning about numbers or shapes	4	4	4
Problems involving real life, money or measures	8	6	8
Handling data			
Organising and using data	5	5	5
Measures, shape and space			
Measures	5	6	5
Reading numbers from scales	1	1	1 ✧
Shape and space	5	4	5
Assess and review	4	4	4
Total (days each term)	**60**	**55**	**60**

To assist mixed Y3/Y4 classes, the number of days allocated to different topics has been kept comparable as far as possible to assist with whole-class planning.

† To be practised daily.

‡ 15 days in total allocated to 'making decisions and checking results'.

✧ Classed as an objective in the Yearly Teaching Programme but listed as a topic for planning purposes.

Allocation of days to topic: Y4

Topic	Number of days		
	Autumn	Spring	Summer
Numbers and the number system			
Place value, ordering and rounding	2	2	2
Counting/properties of numbers/sequences	3	3	3
Fractions and decimals	5	5	5
Calculations			
Understanding addition/subtraction	2	1	2
Rapid recall of addition and subtraction facts	0	0	0 †
Mental calculation strategies + / −	1	1	1
Pencil and paper procedures + / −	5	3	5
Understanding multiplication/division	1	2	1
Rapid recall of multiplication/division facts	0	0	0 †
Mental calculation strategies × / ÷	2	1	2
Pencil and paper procedures × /÷	3	4	3
Checking results of calculations	4	3	4 ‡
Solving problems			
Making decisions	0	0	0 ‡
Reasoning about numbers or shapes	4	4	4
Problems involving real life, money and measures	8	6	8
Handling data			
Organising and interpreting data	5	5	5
Measures, shape and space			
Measures	5	6	5
Reading numbers from scales	1	1	1 ✧
Shape and space	5	4	5
Assess and review	4	4	4
Total (days each term)	**60**	**55**	**60**

To assist with Y4/Y5 classes, the number of days allocated to different topics has been kept comparable as far as possible to assist with whole-class planning.

† To be practised daily.

‡ 11 days in total allocated to 'making decisions and checking results'.

✧ Classed as an objective in the Yearly Teaching Programme but listed as a topic for planning purposes.

STEPS
MATHEMATICS

Allocation of days to topic: Y5

Topic	Number of days		
	Autumn	**Spring**	**Summer**
Numbers and the number system			
Place value, ordering and rounding	2	2	2
Properties of numbers and number sequences	3	3	3
Fractions, decimals/percentages, ratio/proportion	10	5	10
Calculations			
Rapid recall of addition and subtraction facts	0	0	0 †
Mental calculation strategies + / −	1	3	1
Pencil and paper procedures + / −	2	2	2
Understanding multiplication/division	1	1	1
Rapid recall of multiplication/division facts	0	0	0 †
Mental calculation strategies × / ÷	1	1	1
Pencil and paper procedures × / ÷	3	3	3
Using a calculator	4	2	4
Checking results of calculations	3	3	3 ‡
Solving problems			
Making decisions	0	0	0 ‡
Reasoning and generalising about numbers/shapes	3	5	3
Problems involving real life, money and measures	6	7	6
Handling data			
Organising and interpreting data	5	5	5
Measures, shape and space			
Measures	8	4	8
Shape and space	4	5	4
Assess and review	4	4	4
Total (days each term)	**60**	**55**	**60**

To assist mixed Y5/Y6 classes, the number of days allocated to different topics has been kept comparable as far as possible to assist with whole-class planning.

† To be practised daily.

‡ 9 days in total allocated to 'making decisions and checking results including using a calculator'.

Allocation of days to topic: Y6

Topic	Number of days		
	Autumn	**Spring**	**Summer**
Numbers and the number system			
Place value, ordering and rounding	2	2	2
Properties of numbers and number sequences	3	3	3
Fractions, decimals/percentages, ratio/proportion	10	5	10
Calculations			
Mental calculation strategies + / −	1	3	1
Pencil and paper procedures + / −	2	2	2
Understanding multiplication/division	1	1	1
Rapid recall of multiplication/division facts	0	0	0 †
Mental calculation strategies × / ÷	1	1	1
Pencil and paper procedures × / ÷	3	3	3
Using a calculator	4	2	4
Checking results of calculations	3	3	3 ‡
Solving problems			
Making decisions	0	0	0 ‡
Reasoning and generalising about numbers/shapes	3	5	3
Problems involving real life, money and measures	6	7	6
Handling data			
Organising and interpreting data	5	5	5
Measures, shape and space			
Measures	8	4	8
Shape and space	4	5	4
Assess and review	4	4	4
Total (days each term)	60	55	60

To assist mixed Y5/Y6 classes, the number of days allocated to different topics has been kept comparable as far as possible to assist with whole-class planning.

† To be practised daily.

‡ 9 days in total allocated to 'making decisions and checking results including using a calculator'.

Key objectives: Class Record Sheets (R–Y6)

The Framework states that it 'is not necessary or even feasible to check and record each pupil's individual progress against every single teaching objective in mathematics'. Medium-term assessments should focus on the most important aspects of mathematics identified as key objectives. This section is intended to help teachers to keep easily a record of whether each child has achieved the key objectives, and if so, when.

The records will help teachers to track quickly which pupils are in need of further assistance, and also to assess whether there is an objective which it would be beneficial to cover again with the whole class or a smaller group of pupils.

Coordinator's notes

Photocopiable Class Record Sheets for years R to Y6 are included on CM24 to CM30 which provide space for recording the attainments of 12 children.
A continuation sheet is provided on CM31 on which the teacher will need to rule horizontal lines to align with those on the relevant Class Record.

The importance of key objectives

Level descriptions

Key objectives are central to children's progress in relation to the National Curriculum level descriptions and hence to their performance in tests and teacher assessments.

Identifying key objectives

These are listed separately in Section 2 of the Framework and shown in bold in the Teaching Programme for each year group.

Individual targets for pupils

Targets will generally be linked to key objectives which are the focus for your teaching during the next phase of medium-term planning.

Parental involvement

Your class record of key objectives and any supplementary notes can be used to inform parents of and involve parents in their child's progress.

Homework

The key objectives may help provide a focus for homework, e.g. work related to individual targets can be given for homework.

Long-term assessments

Your class record of key objectives and supplementary notes will:

- help you assess/review pupils' progress against school and national targets at the end of each year;
- inform the next teacher of children's responses during that year.

Class records of key objectives

The Framework suggests that:

- half-termly assessments should centre on the key objectives for that half-term and help you to identify children's particular strengths and weaknesses based on your planned expectations;

- children's progress towards the key objectives needs to be recorded, e.g. through a class record;

- records should be updated at least every half-term, e.g. after 'assess and review' days;

- informal notes based on continuous short-term assessments can be written and used;

- supplementary notes, perhaps supported by samples of work, should be kept on individual pupils whose progress towards the key objectives is significantly different from the majority of the class;

- class records are kept in a folder together with supplementary notes to pass on the next teacher at the end of the year.

Class Record for Reception: Key objectives

Class: Teacher: Academic year:

Names												

Key objectives

Say and use the number names in order in familiar contexts.												
Count reliably up to 10 everyday objects.												
Recognise numerals 1 to 9.												
Use language such as more or less, greater or smaller, heavier or lighter, to compare two numbers or quantities.												
In practical activities and discussion, begin to use the vocabulary involved in adding and subtracting.												
Find one more or one less than a number from 1 to 10.												
Begin to relate addition to combining two groups of objects, and subtraction to 'taking away'.												
Talk about, recognise and recreate simple patterns.												
Use language such as circle or bigger to describe the shape and size of solids and flat shapes.												
Use everyday words to describe position.												
Use developing mathematical ideas and methods to solve practical problems.												

- Write the date in the appropriate box when a child has achieved a key objective.
- Write **S** in a box to indicate that supplementary notes have been kept on a child whose progress towards the key objectives is significantly different from the majority of the class.

Class Record for Year 1: Key objectives

Class: Teacher: Academic year:

Names													63

Key objectives

Key objectives													
Count reliably at least 20 objects													
Count on and back in ones from any small number, and in tens from and back to zero.													
Read, write and order numbers from 0 to at least 20; understand and use the vocabulary of comparing and ordering these numbers.													
Within the range of 0 to 30, say the number that is 1 or 10 more or less than any given number.													
Understand the operation of addition, and of subtraction (as 'take away' or 'difference'), and use the related vocabulary.													
Know by heart all pairs of numbers with a total of 10.													
Use mental strategies to solve simple problems using counting, addition, subtraction, doubling and halving, explaining methods of reasoning orally.													
Compare two lengths, masses or capacities by direct comparison.													
Suggest suitable standard or uniform non-standard units and measuring equipment to estimate, then measure, a length, mass or capacity.													
Use everyday language to describe features of familiar 3-D and 2-D shapes.													

- Write the date in the appropriate box when a child has achieved a key objective.
- Write **S** in a box to indicate that supplementary notes have been kept on a child whose progress towards the key objectives is significantly different from the majority of the class.

Class Record for Year 2: Key objectives

Class:　　　　　Teacher:　　　　　Academic year:

Names

Key objectives

Key objectives											
Count, read, write and order whole numbers to at least 100; know what each digit represents (including 0 as a place holder).											
Describe and extend simple number sequences (including odd/even numbers, counting on or back in ones or tens from any two-digit number, and so on).											
Understand that subtraction is the inverse of addition; state the subtraction corresponding to a given addition and vice versa.											
Know by heart all addition and subtraction facts for each number to at least 10.											
Use knowledge that addition can be done in any order to do mental calculations more efficiently.											
Understand the operation of multiplication as repeated addition or as describing an array.											
Know and use halving as the inverse of doubling.											
Know by heart facts for the 2 and 10 multiplication tables.											
Estimate, measure and compare lengths, masses and capacities, using standard units; suggest suitable units and equipment for such measurements.											
Read a simple scale to the nearest labelled division, including using a ruler to draw and measure lines to the nearest centimetre.											
Use the mathematical names for common 2-D and 3-D shapes; sort shapes and describe some of their features.											
Use mathematical vocabulary to describe position, direction and movement.											
Choose and use appropriate operations and efficient calculation strategies to solve problems, explaining how the problem was solved.											

- Write the date in the appropriate box when a child has achieved a key objective.
- Write **S** in a box to indicate that supplementary notes have been kept on a child whose progress towards the key objectives is significantly different from the majority of the class.

Class Record for Year 3: Key objectives

Class: Teacher: Academic year:

Names

Key objectives

Key objectives												
Read, write and order whole numbers to at least 1000; know what each digit represents.												
Count on or back in tens or hundreds from any two- or three-digit number.												
Recognise unit fractions such as $\frac{1}{2}$, $\frac{1}{3}$, $\frac{1}{4}$, $\frac{1}{5}$, $\frac{1}{10}$, and use them to find fractions of shapes and numbers.												
Know by heart all addition and subtraction facts for each number to 20.												
Add and subtract mentally a 'near multiple of 10' to or from a two-digit number.												
Know by heart facts for the 2, 5 and 10 multiplication tables.												
Understand division and recognise that division is the inverse of multiplication.												
Use units of time and know the relationships between them (second, minute, hour, day, week, month, year).												
Understand and use £.p notation.												
Choose and use appropriate operations (including multiplication and division) to solve word problems, explaining methods and reasoning.												
Identify right angles.												
Identify lines of symmetry in simple shapes and recognise shapes with no lines of symmetry.												
Solve a given problem by organising and interpreting numerical data in simple lists, tables and graphs.												

- Write the date in the appropriate box when a child has achieved a key objective.
- Write **S** in a box to indicate that supplementary notes have been kept on a child whose progress towards the key objectives is significantly different from the majority of the class.

Class Record for Year 4: Key objectives

Class: Teacher: Academic year:

Names												

Key objectives

Use symbols correctly, including less than ($<$), greater than ($>$), equals ($=$).												
Round any positive integer less than 1000 to the nearest 10 or 100.												
Recognise simple fractions that are several parts of a whole and mixed numbers; recognise the equivalence of simple fractions.												
Use known number facts and place value to add or subtract mentally, including any pair of two-digit whole numbers												
Carry out column addition and subtraction of two integers less than 1000, and column addition of more than two such integers.												
Know by heart facts for the 2, 3, 4, 5 and 10 multiplication tables.												
Derive quickly division facts corresponding to the 2, 3, 4, 5 and 10 multiplication tables.												
Find remainders after division.												
Know and use the relationship between familiar units of length, mass and capacity.												
Classify polygons, using criteria such as number of right angles, whether or not they are regular, symmetry properties.												
Choose/use appropriate number operations and ways of calculating (mental, mental with jottings, pencil and paper) to solve problems.												

- Write the date in the appropriate box when a child has achieved a key objective.
- Write **S** in a box to indicate that supplementary notes have been kept on a child whose progress towards the key objective is significantly different from the majority of the class.

Class Record for Year 5: Key objectives

Class: Teacher: Academic year:

Names

Key objectives

Key objectives														
Multiply and divide any positive integer up to 10 000 by 10 or 100 and understand the effect.														
Order a given set of positive and negative integers.														
Use decimal notation for tenths and hundredths.														
Round a number with one or two decimal places to the nearest integer.														
Relate fractions to division and to their decimal representations.														
Calculate mentally a difference such as $8006 - 2993$.														
Carry out column addition and subtraction of positive integers less than 10 000.														
Know by heart all multiplication facts up to 10×10.														
Carry out short multiplication and division of a three-digit by a single-digit integer.														
Carry out long multiplication of a two-digit by a two-digit integer.														
Understand area measured in square centimetres (cm²); understand and use the formula in words 'length × breadth' for the area of a rectangle.														
Recognise parallel and perpendicular lines, and properties of rectangles.														
Use all four operations to solve simple word problems involving numbers and quantities, including time, explaining methods and reasoning.														

- Write the date in the appropriate box when a child has achieved a key objective.
- Write **S** in a box to indicate that supplementary notes have been kept on a child whose progress towards the key objectives is significantly different from the majority of the class.

Class Record for Year 6: Key objectives

Class: Teacher: Academic year:

Names										

Key objectives

Multiply and divide decimals mentally by 10 or 100, and integers by 1000, and explain the effect.										
Order a mixed set of numbers with up to three decimal places.										
Reduce a fraction to its simplest form by cancelling common factors.										
Use a fraction as an operator to find fractions of numbers or quantities (e.g. $\frac{5}{8}$ or 32, $\frac{7}{10}$ or 40, $\frac{9}{100}$ of 400 centimetres).										
Understand percentage as the number of parts in every 100, and find simple percentages of small whole-number quantities.										
Solve simple problems involving ratio and proportion.										
Carry out column addition and subtraction of numbers involving decimals.										
Derive quickly division facts corresponding to multiplication tables up to 10 × 10.										
Carry out short multiplication and division of numbers involving decimals.										
Carry out long multiplication of a three-digit by a two-digit integer.										
Use a protractor to measure acute and obtuse angles to the nearest degree.										
Calculate the perimeter and area of simple compound shapes that can be split into rectangles.										
Read and plot co-ordinates in all four quadrants.										
Identify and use the appropriate operations (including combinations of operations) to solve word problems involving numbers and quantities, and explain methods and reasoning.										
Solve a problem by extracting and interpreting information presented in tables, graphs and charts.										

- Write the date in the appropriate box when a child has achieved a key objective.
- Write **S** in a box to indicate that supplementary notes have been kept on a child whose progress towards the key objective is significantly different from the majority of the class.

  **STEPS** MATHEMATICS *Numeracy Coordinator's Handbook*

ames

																			69

Write the date in the appropriate box when a child has achieved a key objective.

Write **S** in a box to indicate that supplementary notes have been kept on a child whose progress towards the key objectives is significantly different from the majority of the class.

Correlation to the Framework

How to use this chart

This chart details how the STEPS Mathematics scheme relates to the National Numeracy Framework. The objectives within each year group of the National Numeracy Framework are clearly referenced to units within the STEPS materials. For example, a reference to STEPS 2: 15 relates to Unit 15 of the STEPS 2 materials (for both teachers and children).

STEPS provides excellent coverage of the National Numeracy Framework's objectives. The STEPS philosophy is also very much in line with that advocated in The National Numeracy Strategy in that:

■ STEPS places an emphasis on developing mental strategies for calculations

■ the STEPS approach is centred on interactive whole class teaching with a wealth of ideas for whole-class, individual and group work

No references within STEPS are given for some of the more general objectives within the Framework as these are covered as an integral part of the scheme. It has also not been possible to provide references for some of the very specific mental calculation strategies as they are not all covered in isolation within STEPS.

It will be necessary to revisit some units more than once so it is important that your planning addresses which activities within a unit you have used to cover a specific objective.

This chart is intended as an overview to working with STEPS alongside the Numeracy Framework.

Index

Note: Key objectives are highlighted in **bold type**.

Yearly Teaching Programme: Reception

Topics	Objectives	STEPS Teacher's Handbook Reference

■ Counting and recognising numbers

Topics	Objectives	STEPS Teacher's Handbook Reference
Counting	**Say and use the number names in order in familiar contexts** such as number rhymes, songs, stories, counting games and activities (first to five, then ten, then twenty and beyond)	**1**: 6, 8, 15, 18, 20, 22 **2**: 9
	Recite the number names in order, continuing the count forwards or backwards from a given number	**1**: 6, 8, 15, 18, 22 **2**: 9
	Count reliably up to 10 everyday objects (first to 5, then 10, then beyond), giving just one number name to each object. Recognise small numbers without counting	**1**: 6, 8, 18, 20 **2**: 9
	Begin to recognise 'none' and 'zero' in stories, rhymes and when counting	**1**: 15, 22
	Count reliably in other contexts, such as clapping sounds or hopping movements	
	Count in tens	**2**: 21
	Count in twos	**2**: 21
	Estimate a number in the range that can be counted reliably, then check by counting	**1**: 20
Reading and writing numbers	**Recognise numerals 1 to 9**, then 0 and 10, then beyond 10	**1**: 6, 8, 18, 20
	Begin to record numbers, initially by making marks, progressing to simple tallying and writing numerals	**1**: 8, 20
Comparing and ordering numbers	**Use language such as more or less, greater or smaller, to compare two numbers** and say which is more or less, and say a number which lies between two given numbers	**1**: 6, 8, 18, 20, 22 **2**: 39
	Order a given set of numbers: for example, the set of numbers 1 to 6 given in random order	**1**: 8, 20, 22 **2**: 39
	Order a given set of selected numbers: for example, the set 2, 5, 1, 8, 4	**1**: 22 **2**: 39
	Begin to understand and use ordinal numbers in different contexts	**1**: 13, 33

■ Adding and subtracting

Topics	Objectives	STEPS Teacher's Handbook Reference
Adding and subtracting in practical activities and discussion	**Begin to use the vocabulary involved in adding and subtracting**	**1**: 11, 24, 29, 31, 35 **2**: 1
	Find one more or one less than a number from 1 to 10	**1**: 11, 16, 22
	Begin to relate addition to combining two groups of objects, counting all the objects; extend to three groups of objects	**1**: 11, 24, 29
	Begin to relate addition to counting on	**1**: 11, 24, 29
	Begin to relate the addition of doubles to counting on	
	Find a total by counting on when one group of objects is hidden	

Topics	Objectives	STEPS Teacher's Handbook Reference
Adding and subtracting in practical activities and discussion *continued*	Separate (partition) a given number of objects into two groups	**1**: 16, 29, 31
	Select two groups of objects to make a given total	**1**: 11, 24, 29
	Begin to relate subtraction to 'taking away' and counting how many are left	**1**: 16, 35
	Remove a smaller number from a larger and find how many are left by counting back from the larger number	**1**: 35 **2**: 3
	Begin to find out how many have been removed from a larger group of objects by counting up from a number	**2**: 3
	Work out by counting how many more are needed to make a larger number	**1**: 31, 35

■ Solving problems

Reasoning about numbers or shapes	**Talk about, recognise and recreate simple patterns**: for example, simple repeating or symmetrical patterns from different cultures	**1**: 10, 28 **2**: 4
	Solve simple problems or puzzles in a practical context, and respond to 'What could we try next?'	
	Make simple estimates and predictions: for example, of the number of cubes that will fit in a box or strides across the room	
	Sort and match objects, pictures or children themselves, justifying the decision made	**1**: 1, 3, 34
Problems involving 'real life' or money	**Use developing mathematical ideas and methods to solve practical problems** involving counting and comparing in a real or role play context	Opportunities throughout all sections in STEPS 1
	Begin to understand and use the vocabulary related to money. Sort coins, including the £1 and £2 coins, and use them in role play to pay and give change	**1**: 25 **2**: 17

■ Measures, shape and space

Comparing and ordering measures	**Use language such as more or less, longer or shorter, heavier or lighter... to compare two quantities**, then more than two, by making direct comparisons of lengths or masses, and by filling and emptying containers	**1**: 4, 7, 9, 17, 19, 32, 36
	Begin to understand and use the vocabulary of time Sequence familiar events Begin to know the days of the week in order Begin to read o'clock time	**1**: 5, 23 **2**: 16, 25, 38
Exploring pattern, shape and space	**Use language such as circle or bigger to describe the shape and size of solids and flat shapes** Begin to name solids such as a cube, cone, sphere... and flat shapes such as a circle, triangle, square, rectangle... Use a variety of shapes to make models, pictures and patterns, and describe them	**1**: 2, 14, 27
	Put sets of objects in order of size	**1**: 1, 34

Topics	Objectives	STEPS Teacher's Handbook Reference
Exploring pattern, shape and space *continued*	Talk about, recognise and recreate patterns: for example, simple repeating or symmetrical patterns in the environment (see also Reasoning)	1: 10, 28 2: 4
	Use everyday words to describe position, direction and movement: for example, follow and give instructions about positions, directions and movements in PE and other activities	1: 12, 30

Yearly Teaching Programme: Year 1

Topics	Objectives	STEPS Teacher's Handbook Reference

■ Numbers and the number system

Topics	Objectives	STEPS Teacher's Handbook Reference
Counting, properties of numbers and number sequences	Know the number names and recite them in order to at least 20, from and back to zero	1: 6, 8, 18, 20 2: 9
	Count reliably at least 20 objects	1: 6, 8, 18, 20 2: 9
	Describe and extend number sequences: **count on and back in ones from any small number, and in tens from and back to zero;** count on in twos from zero, then one, and begin to recognise odd or even numbers to about 20 as 'every other number'; count in steps of five from zero to 20 or more, then back again'; begin to count on in steps of 3 from zero	2: 1, 3, 21
Place value and ordering	**Read and write numerals from 0 to at least 20**	1: 8, 20 2: 9
	Begin to know what each digit in a two-digit number represents. Partition a 'teens' number and begin to partition larger two-digit numbers into a multiple of 10 and ones (TU)	2: 7, 11
	Understand and use the vocabulary of comparing and ordering numbers, including ordinal numbers to at least 20 Use the = sign to represent equality Compare two familiar numbers, say which is more or less, and give a number which lies between them	1: 4, 13, 17, 29, 33 2: 11
	Within the range 0 to 30, say the number that is 1 or 10 more or less than any given number	2: 13, 15
	Order numbers to at least 20, and position them on a number track	1: 9, 15, 18, 19, 22, 32, 36 2: 11
Estimating	Understand and use the vocabulary of estimation Give a sensible estimate of a number of objects that can be checked by counting (e.g. up to about 30 objects)	2: 9

Topics	Objectives	STEPS Teacher's Handbook Reference

▪ Calculations

Topics	Objectives	STEPS Teacher's Handbook Reference
Understanding addition and subtraction	**Understand the operation of addition, and of subtraction (as 'take away', 'difference', and 'how many more to make'), and use the related vocabulary** Begin to recognise that addition can be done in any order Begin to use the $+$, $-$ and $=$ signs to record mental calculations in a number sentence, and to recognise the use of symbols such as $\square$ or $\triangle$ to stand for an unknown number	**1:** 11, 16, 24, 29, 31, 35 **2:** 1, 3, 6
	Begin to recognise that more than two numbers can be added together	**1:** 11, 24, 29 **2:** 1
Rapid recall of addition and subtraction facts	**Know by heart:** **all pairs of numbers with a total of 10** (e.g. $3 + 7$); addition facts for all pairs of numbers with a total up to at least 5 (e.g. $4 + 4$) Begin to know: addition facts for all pairs of numbers with a total up to at least 10, and the corresponding subtraction facts	**2:** 5, 6
Mental calculation strategies ($+$ and $-$)	Use knowledge that addition can be done in any order to do mental calculations more efficiently. For example: put the larger number first and count on in ones, including beyond 10 (e.g. $7 + 5$); begin to partition into '5 and a bit' when adding 6, 7, 8 or 9, then recombine (e.g. $6 + 8 = 5 + 1 + 5 + 3 = 10 + 4 = 14$)	**1:** 22 **2:** 1, 3
	Identify near doubles, using doubles already known (e.g. $6 + 5$)	**3a:** 14, 16
	Add 9 to single-digit numbers by adding 10 then subtracting 1	**3a:** 14
	Use patterns of similar calculations (e.g. $10 - 0 = 10$, $10 - 1 = 9$, $10 - 2 = 8$...)	**2:** 5, 6
	Use known number facts and place value to add or subtract a pair of numbers mentally within the range 0 to at least 10, then 0 to at least 20	**1:** 11, 16, 24, 29, 31, 35 **2:** 13, 15
	Begin to bridge through 10, and later 20, when adding a single-digit number	Opportunities in **2:**13

▪ Solving problems

Topics	Objectives	STEPS Teacher's Handbook Reference
Making decisions	Choose and use appropriate number operations and mental strategies to solve problems	Opportunities throughout number sections (blue) in STEPS 1 and 2
Reasoning about numbers or shapes	Solve simple mathematical problems or puzzles; recognise and predict from simple patterns and relationships. Suggest extensions by asking 'What if...?' or 'What could I try next?'	**1:**10, 28
	Investigate a general statement about familiar numbers or shapes by finding examples that satisfy it	
	Explain methods and reasoning orally	Opportunities throughout number sections (blue) in STEPS 1 and 2

Topics	Objectives	STEPS Teacher's Handbook Reference
Problems involving 'real life', money or measures	**Use mental strategies to solve simple problems** set in 'real life', money or measurement contexts, **using counting, addition, subtraction, doubling and halving, explaining methods and reasoning orally**	Opportunities throughout all sections in STEPS 1 and 2 including **1**: 26 (halving)
	Recognise coins of different values Find totals and change from up to 20p Work out how to pay an exact sum using smaller coins	**1**: 25 **2**: 17
Organising and using data	Solve a given problem by sorting, classifying and organising information in simple ways, such as: using objects or pictures; in a list or simple table Discuss and explain results	**1**: 34, 37 **2**: 22, 40

▧ Measures, shape and space

Measures	Understand and use the vocabulary related to length, mass and capacity **Compare two lengths, masses or capacities by direct comparison;** extend to more than two Measure using uniform non-standard units (e.g. straws, wooden cubes, plastic weights, yogurt pots), or standard units (e.g. metre sticks, litre jugs)	**1**: 4, 7, 9, 17, 19, 21, 32, 36
	Suggest suitable standard or uniform non-standard units and measuring equipment to estimate, then measure, a length, mass or capacity, recording estimates and measurements as 'about 3 beakers full' or 'about as heavy as 20 cubes'	**2**: 10, 12, 14, 18
	Understand and use the vocabulary related to time. Order familiar events in time Know the days of the week and the seasons of the year Read the time to the hour or half hour on analogue clocks	**1**: 5, 23 **2**: 16, 25, 38
Shape and space	**Use everyday language to describe features of familiar 3-D and 2-D shapes,** including the cube, cuboid, sphere, cylinder, cone..., circle, triangle, square, rectangle..., referring to properties such as the shapes of flat faces, or the number of faces or corners... or the number and types of sides	**1**: 2, 14, 27 **2**: 2, 27
	Make and describe models, patterns and pictures using construction kits, everyday materials, Plasticine... Fold shapes in half, then make them into symmetrical patterns Begin to relate solid shapes to pictures of them	**1**: 2, 10, 14, 28 **2**: 2, 24, 27, 35
	Use everyday language to describe position, direction and movement	**1**: 12, 30
	Talk about things that turn Make whole turns and half turns Use one or more shapes to make, describe and continue repeating patterns...	**1**: 10, 12, 28, 30 **2**: 20

Yearly Teaching Programme: Year 2

Topics	Objectives	STEPS Teacher's Handbook Reference

▨ Numbers and the number system

Topics	Objectives	STEPS Teacher's Handbook Reference
Counting, properties of numbers and number sequences	Say the number names in order to at least 100, from and back to zero	2: 24
	Count reliably up to 100 objects by grouping them: for example, in tens, then in fives or twos	2: 24, 39
	Describe and extend simple number sequences: count on or back in ones or tens, starting from any two-digit number; count in hundreds from and back to zero; count on in twos from and back to zero or any small number, and **recognise odd and even numbers** to at least 30; count on in steps of 3, 4 or 5 to at least 30, from and back to zero, then from and back to any given small number	2: 21
	Begin to recognise two-digit multiples of 2, 5 or 10	3a: 12
Place value and ordering	**Read and write whole numbers to at least 100** in figures and words	2: 39
	Know what each digit in a two-digit number represents, including 0 as a place holder, and partition two-digit numbers into a multiple of ten and ones (TU)	2: 7, 11, 24
	Use and begin to read the vocabulary of comparing and ordering numbers, including ordinal numbers to 100 Use the = sign to represent equality Compare two given two-digit numbers, say which is more or less, and give a number which lies between them	2: 39 3a: 5
	Say the number that is 1 or 10 more or less than any given two-digit number	3a: 5
	Order whole numbers to at least 100, and position them on a number line and 100 square	2: 39
Estimating and rounding	Use and begin to read the vocabulary of estimation and approximation; give a sensible estimate of at least 50 objects	2: 24 3a: 5
	Round numbers less than 100 to the nearest 10	3a: 5
Fractions	Begin to recognise and find one half and one quarter of shapes and small numbers of objects Begin to recognise that two halves or four quarters make one whole and that two quarters and one half are equivalent	2: 34

▨ Calculations

Topics	Objectives	STEPS Teacher's Handbook Reference
Understanding addition and subtraction	Extend understanding of the operations of addition and subtraction Use and begin to read the related vocabulary Use the +, − and = signs to record mental additions and subtractions in a number sentence, and recognise the use of a symbol such as □ or △ to stand for an unknown number Recognise that addition can be done in any order, but not subtraction: for example, $3 + 21 = 21 + 3$, but $21 - 3 \neq 3 - 21$	2: 13, 15, 29, 36 3a: 7, 9

Topics	Objectives	STEPS Teacher's Handbook Reference
Understanding addition and subtraction *continued*	Understand that more than two numbers can be added Begin to add three single-digit numbers mentally (totals up to about 20) or three two-digit numbers with the help of apparatus (totals up to 100)	**2:** 29
	Understand that subtraction is the inverse of addition (subtraction reverses addition)	**3a:** 16
Rapid recall of addition and subtraction facts	**Know by heart:** **all addition and subtraction facts for each number to at least 10;** all pairs of numbers with a total of 20 (e.g. 13 + 7, 6 + 14); all pairs of multiples of 10 with a total of 100 (e.g. 30 + 70)	**2:** 13, 15, 29, 36 **3a:** 14
Mental calculation strategies (+ and −)	**Use knowledge that addition can be done in any order to do mental calculations more efficiently.** For example: put the larger number first and count on in tens or ones; add three small numbers by putting the largest number first and/or find a pair totalling 10; partition into '5 and a bit' when adding 6, 7, 8 or 9, then recombine (e.g. 16 + 8 = 15 + 1 + 5 + 3 = 20 + 4 = 24); partition additions into tens and units, then recombine	**3a:** 7, 9, 14, 16
	Find a small difference by counting up from the smaller to the larger number (e.g. 42 − 39)	**3a:** 9
	Identify near doubles, using doubles already known (e.g. 8 + 9, 40 + 41)	**3a:** 14, 16
	Add/subtract 9 or 11: add/subtract 10 and adjust by 1 Begin to add/subtract 19 or 21: add/subtract 20 and adjust by 1	**3a:** 14, 16
	Use patterns of similar calculations	**3a:** 14, 16
	State the subtraction corresponding to a given addition, and vice versa	**3a:** 16
	Use known number facts and place value to add/subtract mentally	**2:** 19, 36
	Bridge through 10 or 20, then adjust	Opportunities in **3a:** 7, 9
Understanding multiplication and division	**Understand the operation of multiplication as repeated addition or as describing an array,** and begin to understand division as grouping (repeated subtraction) or sharing Use and begin to read the related vocabulary Use the ×, ÷ and = signs to record mental calculations in a number sentence, and recognise the use of a symbol such as □ or △ to stand for an unknown number	**2:** 19, 23 **3a:** 1, 3, 12, 24
	Know and use halving as the inverse of doubling	**3a:** 12, 14
Rapid recall of multiplication and division facts	**Know by heart:** **multiplication facts for the 2 and 10 times-tables;** **doubles of all numbers to 10 and the corresponding halves** Begin to know: multiplication facts for the 5 times-table	**3a:** 12, 14
	Derive quickly: division facts corresponding to the 2 and 10 times-tables; doubles of all numbers to at least 15 (e.g. 11 + 11 or 11 × 2); doubles of multiples of 5 to 50 (e.g. 20 × 2 or 35 × 2); halves of multiples of 10 to 100 (e.g. half of 70)	**3a:** 12, 14

Topics	Objectives	STEPS Teacher's Handbook Reference
Mental calculation strategies × and ÷	Use known number facts and place value to carry out mentally simple multiplications and divisions	**3a:** 3, 24
Checking results of calculations	Repeat addition in a different order	**3a:** 1, 5, 41
	Check with an equivalent calculation	**3a:** 1, 5, 41

▓ Solving problems

Making decisions	**Choose and use appropriate operations and efficient calculation strategies** (e.g. mental, mental with jottings) **to solve problems**	Opportunities throughout number sections (blue) in STEPS 2 and 3a
Reasoning about numbers or shapes	Solve mathematical problems or puzzles, recognise simple patterns and relationships, generalise and predict. Suggest extensions by asking 'What if...?' or 'What could I try next?'	**3a:** 14, 16, 18
	Investigate a general statement about familiar numbers or shapes by finding examples that satisfy it	**3a:** 14, 16, 18
	Explain how a problem was solved orally, and where appropriate, in writing	**3a:** 7, 9
Problems involving 'real life', money or measures	Use mental addition and subtraction, simple multiplication and division, to solve simple word problems involving numbers in 'real life', money or measures, using one or two steps. Explain how the problem was solved	Opportunities throughout all sections in STEPS 2 and 3a
	Recognise all coins and begin to use £.p notation for money (for example, know that £4.65 indicates £4 and 65p) Find totals, give change, and work out which coins to pay	**2:** 41 **3a:** 10, 36
Organising and using data	Solve a given problem by sorting, classifying and organising information in simple ways, such as: in a list or simple table; in a pictogram; in a block graph Discuss and explain results	**2:** 22, 32, 40

▓ Measures, shape and space

Measures	Use and begin to read the vocabulary related to length, mass and capacity	**2:** 10, 12, 14, 18
	Estimate, measure and compare lengths, masses and capacities, using standard units (m, cm, kg, litre); **suggest suitable units and equipment for such measurements**	**2:** 10, 12, 14, 18, 26, 28, 31
	Read a simple scale to the nearest labelled division, including using a ruler to draw and measure lines to the nearest centimetre, recording estimates and measurements as '3 and a bit metres long' or 'about 8 centimetres' or 'nearly 3 kilograms heavy'	**2:** 26, 28, 31
	Use and begin to read the vocabulary related to time Use units of time and know the relationships between them (second, minute, hour, day, week) Suggest suitable units to estimate or measure time Order the months of the year Read the time to the hour, half hour or quarter hour on an analogue clock and a 12-hour digital clock, and understand the notation 7:30	**2:** 16, 25, 38

Topics	Objectives	STEPS Teacher's Handbook Reference
Shape and space	**Use the mathematical names for common 3-D and 2-D shapes,** including the pyramid, cylinder, pentagon, hexagon, octagon...	
	Sort shapes and describe some of their features, such as the number of sides and corners, symmetry (2-D shapes), or the shapes of faces and number of faces, edges and corners (3-D shapes)	**2:** 2, 8, 27, 33 **3a:** 21, 33
	Make and describe shapes, pictures and patterns, using for example, solid shapes, templates, pinboard and elastic bands, squared paper, a programmable robot... Relate solid shapes to pictures of them	**3a:** 38
	Begin to recognise line symmetry	**2:** 4 **3a:** 2
	Use mathematical vocabulary to describe position, direction and movement: for example, describe, place, tick, draw or visualise objects in given positions	**1:** 30 **2:** 20
	Recognise whole, half and quarter turns, to the left or right, clockwise or anti-clockwise Know that a right angle is a measure of a quarter turn, and recognise right angles in squares and rectangles Give instructions for moving along a route in straight lines and round right-angled corners: for example, to pass through a simple maze...	**2:** 20, 30, 37 **3a:** 8 **3b:** 13

Yearly Teaching Programme: Year 3

Topics	Objectives	STEPS Teacher's Handbook Reference

■ Numbers and the number system

Topics	Objectives	STEPS Teacher's Handbook Reference
Counting, properties of numbers and number sequences	Count larger collections by grouping them: for example, in tens, then other numbers	
	Describe and extend number sequences: **count on or back in tens or hundreds, starting from any two- or three-digit number;** count on or back in twos starting from any two-digit number, and recognise odd and even numbers to at least 100; count on in steps of 3, 4 or 5 from any small number to at least 50, then back again	**3a:** 5, 18
	Recognise two-digit and three-digit multiples of 2, 5 or 10, and three-digit multiples of 50 and 100	**3b:** 3, 22
Place value and ordering	**Read and write whole numbers to at least 1000** in figures and words	**3a:** 5, 17 **3b:** 10
	Know what each digit represents, and partition three-digit numbers into a multiple of 100, a multiple of ten and ones (HTU)	**3a:** 5, 17 **3b:** 10
	Read and begin to write the vocabulary of comparing and ordering numbers, including ordinal numbers to at least 100 Compare two given three-digit numbers, say which is more or less, and give a number which lies between them	**3a:** 5, 17

Topics	Objectives	STEPS Teacher's Handbook Reference
Place value and ordering *continued*	Say the number that is 1, 10 or 100 more or less than any given two- or three-digit number	**3a:** 14, 16, 27, 30
	Order whole numbers to at least 1000, and position them on a number line	**3a:** 17
Estimating and rounding	Read and begin to write the vocabulary of estimation and approximation Give a sensible estimate of up to about 100 objects	**3a:** 17
	Round any two-digit number to the nearest 10 and any three-digit number to the nearest 100	**3a:** 5, 17 **3b:** 10
Fractions	**Recognise unit fractions such as $\frac{1}{2}$, $\frac{1}{3}$, $\frac{1}{4}$, $\frac{1}{5}$, $\frac{1}{10}$... and use them to find fractions of shapes and numbers** Begin to recognise simple fractions that are several parts of a whole, such as $\frac{3}{4}$, $\frac{2}{3}$ or $\frac{3}{10}$ Begin to recognise simple equivalent fractions: for example, five tenths and one half, five fifths and one whole Compare familiar fractions: for example, know that on the number line, one half lies between one quarter and three quarters Estimate a simple fraction	**3a:** 23 **3b:** 12

▓ Calculations

Topics	Objectives	STEPS Teacher's Handbook Reference
Understanding addition and subtraction	Extend understanding of the operations of addition and subtraction, read and begin to write the related vocabulary, and continue to recognise that addition can be done in any order Use the $+$, $-$ and $=$ signs	**3a:** 7, 16 **3b:** 11
	Extend understanding that more than two numbers can be added; add three or four single-digit numbers mentally, or three or four two-digit numbers with the help of apparatus or pencil and paper	**3a:** 7, 27
	Extend understanding that subtraction is the inverse of addition	**3b:** 11
Rapid recall of addition and subtraction facts	**Know by heart:** **all addition and subtraction facts for each number to 20;** all pairs of multiples of 100 with a total of 1000 (e.g. 300 + 700) Derive quickly: all pairs of multiples of 5 with a total of 100 (e.g. 35 + 65)	**3b:** 25, 28
Mental calculation strategies (+ and −)	Use knowledge that addition can be done in any order to do mental calculations more efficiently. For example: put the larger number first and count on; add three or four small numbers by putting the largest number first and/or by finding pairs totalling 9, 10 or 11; partition into '5 and a bit' when adding 6, 7, 8 or 9 (e.g. 47 + 8 = 45 + 2 + 5 + 3 = 50 + 5 = 55); partition into tens and units, then recombine (e.g. 34 + 53 = 30 + 50 + 4 + 3)	**3a:** 7, 17, 18
	Find a small difference by counting up from the smaller to the larger number (e.g. 102 − 97)	**3b:** 11
	Identify near doubles, using doubles already known (e.g. 80 + 81)	**3a:** 14, 16
	Add and subtract mentally a 'near multiple of 10' to or from a two-digit number... by adding or subtracting 10, 20, 30... and adjusting	
	Use patterns of similar calculations	**3b:** 25

Topics	Objectives	STEPS Teacher's Handbook Reference
Mental calculation strategies (+ and −) *continued*	Say or write a subtraction statement corresponding to a given addition statement, and vice versa	**3a:** 16
	Use known number facts and place value to add/subtract mentally	**3a:** 9, 27, 30
	Bridge through a multiple of 10, then adjust	**3b:** 25
Pencil and paper procedures (+ and −)	Use informal pencil and paper methods to support, record or explain HTU ± TU, HTU ± HTU Begin to use column addition and subtraction for HTU ± TU where the calculation cannot easily be done mentally	**3a:** 27, 30
Understanding multiplication and division	Understand multiplication as repeated addition Read and begin to write the related vocabulary Extend understanding that multiplication can be done in any order	**2:** 19 **3a:** 1, 12
	Understand division as grouping (repeated subtraction) or sharing Read and begin to write the related vocabulary **Recognise that division is the inverse of multiplication**, and that halving is the inverse of doubling	**3a:** 3, 24
	Begin to find remainders after simple division	**3a:** 3, 24
	Round up or down after division, depending on the context	**3a:** 3, 24
Rapid recall of multiplication and division facts	**Know by heart:** **multiplication facts for the 2, 5 and 10 times-tables** Begin to know the 3 and 4 times-tables	**3b:** 22, 34
	Derive quickly: division facts corresponding to the 2, 5 and 10 times-tables; doubles of all whole numbers to at least 20 (e.g. 17 + 17 or 17 × 2); doubles of multiples of 5 to 100 (e.g. 75 × 2, 90 × 2); doubles of multiples of 50 to 500 (e.g. 450 × 2); and all the corresponding halves (e.g. 36 ÷ 2, half of 130, 900 ÷ 2)	**3a:** 18 **3b:** 27
Mental calculation strategies (× and ÷)	To multiply by 10/100 shift the digits one/two places to the left	**4a:** 1
	Use doubling or halving, starting from known facts (e.g. 8 × 4 is double 4 × 4)	**4a:** 3
	Say or write a division statement corresponding to a given multiplication statement	**3a:** 24
	Use known number facts and place value to carry out mentally simple multiplications and divisions	**3b:** 3, 8
Checking results of calculations	Check subtraction with addition, halving with doubling and division with multiplication	**3b:** 7, 11
	Repeat addition or multiplication in a different order	**3a:** 1
	Check with an equivalent calculation	**3b:** 6

▓ Solving problems

Making decisions	**Choose and use appropriate operations (including multiplication and division) to solve word problems,** and appropriate ways of calculating; mental, mental with jottings, pencil and paper	Opportunities throughout number sections (blue) in STEPS 3a and 3b

Topics	Objectives	STEPS Teacher's Handbook Reference
Reasoning about numbers or shapes	Solve mathematical problems or puzzles, recognise simple patterns and relationships, generalise and predict. Suggest extensions by asking 'What if...?'	**3a**: 18 **3b**: 37, 39
	Investigate a general statement about familiar numbers or shapes by finding examples that satisfy it	Integral throughout
	Explain methods and reasoning orally and, where appropriate, in writing	
Problems involving 'real life', money and measures	Solve word problems involving numbers in 'real life', money and measures, using one or more steps, including finding total and giving change, and working out which coins to pay Explain how the problem was solved	Opportunities throughout all sections in STEPS 3a and 3b
	Recognise all coins and notes. **Understand and use £.p notation** (for example, know that £3.06 is £3 and 6p)	**3a**: 10, 36

▨ Handling data

Topics	Objectives	STEPS Teacher's Handbook Reference
Organising and using data	**Solve a given problem by organising and interpreting numerical data in simple lists, tables and graphs,** for example: simple frequency tables; pictograms – symbols representing two units; bar charts – intervals labelled in ones then twos; Venn and Carroll diagrams (one criterion)	**3a**: 4, 26, 31, 33, 39

▨ Measures, shape and space

Topics	Objectives	STEPS Teacher's Handbook Reference
Measures	Read and begin to write the vocabulary related to length, mass and capacity Measure and compare using standard units (km, m, cm, kg, g, l, ml), including using a ruler to draw and measure lines to the nearest half centimetre Know the relationships between kilometres and metres, metres and centimetres, kilograms and grams, litres and millilitres Begin to use decimal notation for metres and centimetres	**3a**: 6, 11, 15, 20, 25, 29, 34, 35, 37
	Suggest suitable units and measuring equipment to estimate or measure length, mass or capacity	**3a**: 6, 11, 15, 20, 25, 29, 34, 37
	Read scales to the nearest division (labelled or unlabelled) Record estimates and measurements to the nearest whole or half unit (e.g. 'about 3.5 kg'), or in mixed units (e.g. '3 m and 20 cm')	**3a**: 6, 11, 15, 20, 25, 29, 34, 37
	Read and begin to write the vocabulary related to time **Use units of time and know the relationships between them (second, minute, hour, day, week, month, year)** Suggest suitable units to estimate or measure time Use a calendar Read the time to 5 minutes on an analogue clock and a 12-hour digital clock, and use the notation 9:40	**3a**: 22, 40
Shape and space	Classify and describe 3-D and 2-D shapes, including the hemisphere, prism, semi-circle, quadrilateral... referring to properties such as reflective symmetry (2-D), the number or shapes of faces, the number of sides/edges and vertices, whether sides/edges are the same length, whether or not angles are right angles...	**3a**: 19, 21, 38 **3b**: 24, 29

Topics	Objectives	STEPS Teacher's Handbook Reference
Shape and space *continued*	Make and describe shapes and patterns: for example, explore the different shapes that can be made from four cubes Relate solid shapes to pictures of them	**3a:** 13, 19, 21, 28, 32, 35, 38
	Identify and sketch **lines of symmetry in simple shapes, and recognise shapes with no lines of symmetry** Sketch the reflection of a simple shape in a mirror line along one edge	**2:** 4 **3a:** 20
	Read and begin to write the vocabulary related to position, direction and movement: for example, describe and find the position of a square on a grid of squares with the rows and columns labelled Recognise and use the four compass directions N, S, E, W	**3a:** 8 **3b:** 13, 14
	Make and describe right-angled turns, including turns between the four compass points **Identify right angles** in 2-D shapes and the environment Recognise that a straight line is equivalent to two right angles Compare angles with a right angle	**3a:** 8, 19 **3b:** 2, 4

Yearly Teaching Programme: Year 4

Topics	Objectives	STEPS Teacher's Handbook Reference

▨ Numbers and the number system

Topics	Objectives	STEPS Teacher's Handbook Reference
Place value, ordering and rounding (whole numbers)	Read and write whole numbers to at least 10 000 in figures and words, and know what each digit represents Partition numbers into thousands, hundreds, tens and ones	**4a:** 1
	Add/subtract 1, 10, 100 or 1000 to/from any integer, and count on or back in tens, hundreds or thousands from any whole number up to 10 000	
	Multiply or divide any integer up to 1000 by 10 (whole-number answers), and understand the effect Begin to multiply by 100	**4a:** 1
	Read and write the vocabulary of comparing and ordering numbers. **Use symbols correctly, including less than (<), greater than (>), equals (=)** Give one or more numbers lying between two given numbers and order a set of whole numbers less than 10 000	**4a:** 1
	Read and write the vocabulary of estimation and approximation. Make and justify estimates up to about 250, and estimate a proportion. **Round any positive integer less than 1000 to the nearest 10 or 100**	**3b:** 25, 28
	Recognise negative numbers in context (e.g. on a number line, on a temperature scale)	**3b:** 33
Properties of numbers and number sequences	Recognise and extend number sequences formed by counting from any number in steps of constant size, extending beyond zero when counting back: for example, count on in steps of 25 to 500, and then back to, say, –100	

Topics	Objectives	STEPS Teacher's Handbook Reference
Properties of numbers and number sequences *continued*	Recognise odd and even numbers up to 1000, and some of their properties, including the outcome of sums or differences of pairs of odd/even numbers	
	Recognise multiples of 2, 3, 4, 5 and 10, up to the tenth multiple	3b: 3
Fractions and decimals	Use fraction notation. **Recognise simple fractions that are several parts of a whole,** such as $2/3$ or $5/8$, **and mixed numbers,** such as $5\frac{3}{4}$; **recognise the equivalence of simple fractions** (e.g. fractions equivalent to $1/2$, $1/4$ or $3/4$) Identify two simple fractions with a total of 1 (e.g. $3/10$ and $7/10$)	3b: 12 4a: 36
	Order simple fractions: for example, decide whether fractions such as $3/8$ or $7/10$ are greater or less than one half	4a: 36
	Begin to relate fractions to division and find simple fractions such as $1/2$, $1/3$, $1/4$, $1/5$, $1/10$... of numbers or quantities Find fractions such as $2/3$, $3/4$, $3/5$, $7/10$... of shapes	4a: 36
	Begin to use ideas of simple proportion: for example, 'one for every...' and 'one in every...'	
	Understand decimal notation and place value for tenths and hundredths and use it in context. For example: order amounts of money; convert a sum of money such as £13.25 to pence, or a length such as 125 cm to metres; round a sum of money to the nearest pound	3a: 10, 29, 36 3b: 6, 23
	Recognise the equivalence between the decimal and fraction forms of one half and one quarter, and tenths such as 0.3	3a: 29 4a: 9

■ Calculations

Topics	Objectives	STEPS Teacher's Handbook Reference
Understanding addition and subtraction	Consolidate understanding of relationship between + and − Understand the principles (not the names) of the commutative and associative laws as they apply or not to addition and subtraction	3b: 11
Rapid recall of addition and subtraction facts	Consolidate knowing by heart: addition and subtraction facts for all numbers to 20 Derive quickly: all numbers pairs that total 100 (e.g. 62 + 38, 75 + 25, 40 + 60); all pairs of multiples of 50 with a total of 1000 (e.g. 850 + 150)	3a: 7, 9 3b: 25, 28
Mental calculation strategies (+ and −)	Find a small difference by counting up (e.g. 5003 − 4996)	4a: 13
	Count on or back in repeated steps of 1, 10 or 100	Opportunities in 4a: 21
	Partition into tens and units, adding the tens first	
	Identify near doubles, using known doubles (e.g. 150 + 160)	
	Add or subtract the nearest multiple of 10, then adjust	
	Continue to use the relationship between addition and subtraction	4a: 5, 7
	Add 3 or 4 small numbers, finding pairs totalling 10, or 9 or 11 Add three two-digit multiples of 10, such as 40 + 70 + 50	4a: 5, 7
	Use known number facts and place value to add or subtract mentally, including any pair of two-digit whole numbers	4b: 7

Topics	Objectives	STEPS Teacher's Handbook Reference
Pencil and paper procedures (+ and −)	Use informal pencil and paper methods to support, record or explain additions/subtractions **Develop and refine written methods for:** **column addition and subtraction of two whole numbers less than 1000, and addition of more than two such numbers;** money calculations (for example, £7.85 ± £3.49)	**3b:** 6, 11, 36 **4a:** 11, 13, 21
Understanding multiplication and division	Extend understanding of the operations of × and ÷, and their relationship to each other and to + and − Understand the principles (not the names) of the commutative, associative and distributive laws as they apply to multiplication	**4a:** 27
	Find remainders after division Divide a whole number of pounds by 2, 4, 5 or 10 to give £.p. Round up or down after division, depending on the context	**4a:** 23, 24, 30
Rapid recall of multiplication and division facts	**Know by heart:** **multiplication facts for 2, 3, 4, 5 and 10 times-tables**	**3b:** 22, 27, 34
	Begin to know: multiplication facts for 6, 7, 8 and 9 times-tables	**4a:** 19, 23, 27, 30
	Derive quickly: **division facts corresponding to 2, 3, 4, 5 and 10 times-tables:** doubles of all whole numbers to 50 (e.g. 38 + 38, or 38 × 2); doubles of multiples of 10 to 500 (e.g. 460 × 2); doubles of multiples of 100 to 5000 (e.g. 3400 × 2); and the corresponding halves (e.g. 74 + 2, ½ of 420, half of 3800)	**3b:** 22, 27, 34
Mental calculation strategies (× and ÷)	Use doubling or halving, starting from known facts. For example: double/halve two-digit numbers by doubling/halving the tens first; to multiply by 4, double, then double again; to multiply by 5, multiply by 10 then halve; to multiply by 20, multiply by 10 then double; find the 8 times-table facts by doubling the 4 times-table; find quarters by halving halves	**4a:** 1
	Use closely related facts (e.g. to multiply 9 or 11, multiply by 10 and adjust; develop the ×6 table from the ×4 and ×2 tables)	**4a:** 3, 19
	Partition (e.g. 23 × 4 = (20 × 4) + (3 × 4))	**4a:** 27
	Use the relationship between multiplication and division	**4a:** 29
	Use known number facts and place value to multiply and divide integers, including by 10 and then 100 (whole-number answers)	**3b:** 22, 27, 34
Pencil and paper procedures (× and ÷)	Approximate first. Use informal pencil and paper methods to support, record or explain multiplications and divisions Develop and refine written methods for TU × U, TU ÷ U	**4a:** 21, 27, 30
Checking results of calculations	Check with the inverse operation	**3b:** 6 **4a:** 29
	Check the sum of several numbers by adding in reverse order	**3b:** 7
	Check with an equivalent calculation	Opportunities in **4a:** 11, 13
	Estimate and check by approximating (round to nearest 10 or 100)	**3b:** 10, 25, 28
	Use knowledge of sums or differences of odd/even numbers	

Topics	Objectives	STEPS Teacher's Handbook Reference

■ Solving problems

Topics	Objectives	STEPS Teacher's Handbook Reference
Making decisions	**Choose and use appropriate number operations and appropriate ways of calculating (mental, mental with jottings, pencil and paper) to solve problems**	**4a**: 5, 7, 11, 13
Reasoning about numbers and shapes	Explain methods and reasoning orally and in writing	**4a**: 11, 13
	Solve mathematical problems or puzzles, recognise and explain patterns and relationships, generalise and predict Suggest extensions by asking 'What if…?'	**3a**: 39, 41 **3b**: 37, 39
	Make and investigate a general statement about familiar numbers or shapes by finding examples that satisfy it	**4a**: 19
Problems involving 'real life', money and measures	Use all four operations to solve word problems involving numbers in 'real life', money and measures (including time), using one or more steps, including converting pounds to pence and metres to centimetres and vice versa	Opportunities throughout all sections in STEPS 3b and 4a including **3b**: 17, **4a**: 24 (money)

■ Handling data

Topics	Objectives	STEPS Teacher's Handbook Reference
Organising and interpreting data	Solve a problem by collecting quickly, organising, representing and interpreting data in tables, charts, graphs and diagrams, including those generated by a computer, for example: tally charts and frequency tables; pictograms – symbol representing 2, 5, 10 or 20 units; bar charts – intervals labelled in 2s, 5s, 10s or 20s; Venn and Carroll diagrams (two criteria)	**3a**: 33 **3b**: 1, 21, 32, 38 **4a**: 6, 22, 37

■ Measures, shape and space

Topics	Objectives	STEPS Teacher's Handbook Reference
Measures	Use, read and write standard metric units (km, m, cm, mm, kg, g, l, ml), including their abbreviations, and imperial units (mile, pint)	**3a**: 6, 11, 20, 34, 37 **3b**: 9, 16, 18, 30 **4a**: 10, 16, 18
	Know and use the relationships between familiar units of length, mass and capacity Know the equivalent of one half, one quarter, three quarters and one tenth of 1 km, 1 m, 1 kg, 1 litre in m, cm, g, ml. Convert up to 1000 centimetres to metres, and vice versa	**3a**: 6, 11, 20, 34, 37 **3b**: 9, 16, 18, 30 **4a**: 10, 16, 18
	Suggest suitable units and measuring equipment to estimate or measure length, mass or capacity Record estimates and readings from scales to a suitable degree of accuracy	**3a**: 6, 11, 20, 34, 37 **3b**: 9, 16, 18, 30 **4a**: 10, 16, 18
	Measure and calculate the perimeter and area of rectangles and other simple shapes, using counting methods and standard units (cm, cm²)	**3a**: 35 **3b**: 15 **4a**: 15
	Use, read and write the vocabulary related to time Estimate/check times using seconds, minutes, hours Read the time from an analogue clock to the nearest minute, and from a 12-hour digital clock Use am and pm and the notation 9:53 Read simple timetables and use this year's calendar	**3a**: 40 **3b**: 5 **4a**: 4, 26

Topics	Objectives	STEPS Teacher's Handbook Reference
Shape and space	Describe and visualise 3-D and 2-D shapes, including the tetrahedron and heptagon Recognise equilateral and isosceles triangles **Classify polygons using criteria such as number of right angles, whether or not they are regular, symmetry properties**	**3b:** 20, 24, 29 **4a:** 8, 12, 20, 28
	Make shapes: for example, construct polygons by paper folding or using pinboard, and discuss properties such as lines of symmetry Visualise 3-D shapes from 2-D drawings and identify simple nets of solid shapes	**3b:** 19, 20, 24, 29, 31 **4a:** 12, 33
	Sketch the reflection of a simple shape in a mirror line parallel to one side (all sides parallel or perpendicular to the mirror line)	**3b:** 20 **4a:** 25
	Recognise positions and directions: for example, describe and find the position of a point on a grid of squares where the lines are numbered Recognise simple examples of horizontal and vertical lines. Use the eight compass directions N, S, E, W, NE, NW, SE, SW	**3b:** 4, 14, 35 **4b:** 19
	Make and measure clockwise and anti-clockwise turns: for example, from SW to N, or from 4 to 10 on a clock face Begin to know that angles are measured in degrees and that: one whole turn is 360° or 4 right angles; a quarter turn is 90° or one right angle; half a right angle is 45° Start to order a set of angles less than 180°	**3b:** 4, 26, 35 **4a:** 2

Yearly Teaching Programme: Year 5

Topics	Objectives	STEPS Teacher's Handbook Reference

◼ Numbers and the number system

Topics	Objectives	STEPS Teacher's Handbook Reference
Place value, ordering and rounding	Read and write whole numbers in figures and words, and know what each digit represents	**4a:** 21 **4b:** 25
	Multiply and divide any positive integer up to 10 000 by 10 or 100 and understand the effect (e.g. 9900 ÷ 10, 737 ÷ 10, 2060 ÷ 100)	**4b:** 11
	Use the vocabulary of comparing and ordering numbers, including symbols such as <, >, = Give one or more numbers lying between two given numbers. Order a set of integers less than 1 million	**4a:** 21
	Use the vocabulary of estimation and approximation Make and justify estimates of large numbers, and estimate simple proportions such as one third, seven tenths Round any integer up to 10 000 to the nearest 10, 100 or 1000	**4a:** 1, 36
	Order a given set of positive and negative integers (e.g. on a number line, on a temperature scale) Calculate a temperature rise or fall across 0°C	**3b:** 33 **5:** 4

Topics	Objectives	STEPS Teacher's Handbook Reference
Properties of numbers and number sequences	Recognise and extend number sequences formed by counting from any number in steps of constant size, extending beyond zero when counting back. For example: count on in steps of 25 to 1000, and then back; count on or back in steps of 0.1, 0.2, 0.3...	
	Make general statements about odd or even numbers, including the outcome of sums and differences	**4b:** 28
	Recognise multiples of 6, 7, 8, 9 up to the 10th multiple Know and apply tests of divisibility by 2, 4, 5, 10 or 100	**4b:** 1
	Know squares of numbers to at least 10×10	**4b:** 1
	Find all the pairs of factors of any number up to 100	**4b:** 1
Fractions, decimals and percentages, ratio and proportion	Use fraction notation, including mixed numbers, and the vocabulary numerator and denominator Change an improper fraction to a mixed number (e.g. change $^{13}/_{10}$ to $1^3/_{10}$) Recognise when two simple fractions are equivalent, including relating hundredths to tenths (e.g. $^{70}/_{100} = ^7/_{10}$)	**4b:** 4, 18
	Order a set of fractions, such as 2, $2^3/_4$, $1^3/_4$, $2^1/_2$, $1^1/_2$, and position them on a number line	**4a:** 36
	Relate fractions to division, and use division to find simple fractions, including tenths and hundredths, of numbers and quantities (e.g. $^3/_4$ of 12, $^1/_{10}$ of 50, $^1/_{100}$ of £3)	**4a:** 36 **4b:** 16, 18
	Solve simple problems using ideas of ratio and proportion ('one for every...' and 'one in every...')	
	Use decimal notation for tenths and hundredths Know what each digit represents in a number with up to two decimal places Order a set of measurements with the same number of decimal places	**4a:** 17 **4b:** 8
	Round a number with one or two decimal places to the nearest integer	**3b:** 23 **4a:** 17
	Relate fractions to their decimal representations: that is, recognise the equivalence between the decimal and fraction forms of one half, one quarter, three quarters... and tenths and hundredths (e.g. $^7/_{10} = 0.7$, $^{27}/_{100} = 0.27$)	**4b:** 4
	Begin to understand percentage as the number of parts in every 100, and find simple percentages of small whole-number quantities (e.g. 25% of £8) Express one half, one quarter, three quarters, and tenths and hundredths, as percentages (e.g. know that $^3/_4 = 75\%$)	**4a:** 9 **4b:** 4

■ Calculations

Rapid recall of addition and subtraction facts	Derive quickly or continue to derive quickly: decimals that total 1 (e.g. 0.2 + 0.8) or 10 (e.g. 6.2 + 3.8); all two-digit pairs that total 100 (e.g. 43 + 57); all pairs of multiples of 50 with a total of 1000 (e.g. 350 + 650)	
Mental calculation strategies (+ and −)	Find differences by counting up through next multiple of 10, 100 or 1000, e.g. **calculate mentally a difference such as 8006 − 2993**	

Topics	Objectives	STEPS Teacher's Handbook Reference
Mental calculation strategies (+ and −) *continued*	Partition into H, T and U, adding the most significant digits first	
	Identify near doubles, such as 1.5 + 1.6	
	Add or subtract the nearest multiple of 10 or 100, then adjust	**4b**: 4
	Develop further the relationship between addition and subtraction	
	Add several numbers (e.g. four or five single digits, or multiples of 10 such as 40 + 50 + 80)	**4b**: 7
	Use known number facts and place value for mental addition and subtraction (e.g. 470 + 380, 810 − 380, 7.4 + 9.8, 9.2 − 8.6)	
Pencil and paper procedures (+ and −)	Use informal pencil and paper methods to support, record or explain additions and subtractions **Extend written methods to:** **column addition/subtraction of two integers less than 10 000;** addition of more than two integers less than 10 000; addition or subtraction of a pair of decimal fractions, both with one or both with two decimal places (e.g. £29.78 + £53.34)	**4b**: 5, 8, 9, 22
Understanding multiplication and division	Understand the effects of and relationships between the four operations, and the principles (not the names) of the arithmetic laws as they apply to multiplication. Begin to use brackets	**4a**: 19, 29, 30 **4b**: 16
	Begin to express a quotient as a fraction, or as a decimal when dividing a whole number by 2, 4, 5 or 10, or when dividing £.p Round up or down after division, depending on the context	**4b**: 30
Rapid recall of multiplication and division facts	**Know by heart all multiplication facts up to 10 × 10**	**4b**: 1, 28
	Derive quickly or continue to derive quickly: division facts corresponding to tables up to 10 × 10; doubles of all whole numbers 1 to 100 (e.g. 78 × 2); doubles of multiples of 10 to 1000 (e.g. 670 × 2); doubles of multiples of 100 to 10 000 (e.g. 6500 × 2); and the corresponding halves	**4a**: 34 **4b**: 1, 28
Mental calculation strategies (× and ÷)	Use doubling or halving, starting from known facts. For example: double/halve any two-digit number by doubling/halving the tens first; double one number and halve the other; to multiply by 25, multiply by 100 then divide by 4; find the ×16 table facts by doubling the ×8 table; find sixths by halving thirds	**4a**: 34
	Use factors (e.g. 8 × 12 = 8 × 4 × 3)	**4b**: 1
	Use closely related facts (e.g. multiply by 19 or 21 by multiplying by 20 and adjusting; develop the ×12 table from the ×10 and ×2 tables)	
	Partition (e.g. 47 × 6 = (40 × 6) +(7 × 6))	**4b**: 11
	Use the relationship between multiplication and division	**4b**: 30
	Use known facts and place value to multiply and divide mentally	**4b**: 28
Pencil and paper procedures (× and ÷)	Approximate first. Use informal pencil and paper methods to support, record or explain multiplications and divisions **Extend written method to:** **short multiplication of HTU or U.t by U;** **long multiplication of TU by TU;** **short division of HTU by U** (with integer remainder)	**4b**: 11, 16, 30 **5**: 7

Topics	Objectives	STEPS Teacher's Handbook Reference
Using a calculator	Develop calculator skills and use a calculator effectively	Integral throughout
Checking results of calculations	Check with the inverse operation when using a calculator	**4b**: 1, 5, 7, 9, 16
	Check the sum of several numbers by adding in the reverse order	**4b**: 5, 6, 7, 9, 16
	Check with an equivalent calculation	**4b**: 5, 6, 7, 9, 16
	Estimate by approximating (round to nearest 10 or 100), then check result	**4b**: 5, 6, 7, 9, 16
	Use knowledge of sums and differences of odd/even numbers	**4b**: 28

■ Solving problems

Making decisions	Choose and use appropriate number operations to solve problems, and appropriate ways of calculating: mental, mental with jottings, written methods, calculator	**4b**: 5, 9, 11, 16
Reasoning and generalising about numbers or shapes	Explain methods and reasoning, orally and in writing	
	Solve mathematical problems or puzzles, recognise and explain patterns and relationships, generalise and predict Suggest extensions asking 'What if...?'	**4a**: 29 **4b**: 22, 35
	Make and investigate a general statement about familiar numbers or shapes by finding examples that satisfy it Explain a generalised relationship (formula) in words	**4b**: 1
Problems involving 'real life', money and measures	**Use all four operations to solve simple word problems involving numbers and quantities** based on 'real life', money and measures **(including time),** using one or more steps, including making simple conversions of pounds to foreign currency and finding simple percentages **Explain methods and reasoning**	Opportunities throughout all sections in STEPS 4a and 4b including **4a**: 24, **4b**: 22 (money); **4b**: 4 (percentages)

■ Handling data

Organising and interpreting data	Discuss the chance or likelihood of particular events	**3a**: 26 **3b**: 21 **4b**: 15
	Solve a problem by representing and interpreting data in tables, charts, graphs and diagrams, including those generated by a computer, for example: bar line charts, vertical axis labelled in 2s, 5s, 10s, 20s or 100s, first where intermediate points have no meaning (e.g. scores on a dice rolled 50 times), then where they may have meaning (e.g. room temperature over time)	**4a**: 6, 32, 37 **4b**: 13, 15, 27, 33
	Find the mode of a set of data	**4b**: 21

Topics	Objectives	STEPS Teacher's Handbook Reference

▦ Measures, shape and space

Topics	Objectives	STEPS Teacher's Handbook Reference
Measures	Use, read and write standard metric units (km, m, cm, mm, kg, g, l, ml), including their abbreviations, and relationships between them. Convert larger to smaller units (e.g. km to m, m to cm or mm, kg to g, l to ml) Know imperial units (mile, pint, gallon)	4a: 10, 16, 35 4b: 8, 20
	Suggest suitable units and measuring equipment to estimate or measure length, mass or capacity Measure and draw lines to the nearest millimetre Record estimates and readings from scales to a suitable degree of accuracy	4a: 10, 16, 35 4b: 8, 20
	Understand area measured in square centimetres (cm²) **Understand and use the formula in words 'length × breadth' for the area of a rectangle** Understand, measure and calculate perimeters of rectangles and regular polygons	3a: 25 3b: 18 4a: 15, 18 4b: 2
	Use units of time: read the time on a 24-hour digital clock and use 24-hour clock notation, such as 19:53. Use timetables	4a: 4, 26 4b: 34
Shape and space	**Recognise properties of rectangles** Classify triangles (isosceles, equilateral, scalene), using criteria such as equal sides, equal angles, lines of symmetry	4a: 8
	Make shapes with increasing accuracy Visualise 3-D shapes from 2-D drawings and identify different nets for an open cube	3b: 24, 29 4a: 12, 28 4b: 6, 10, 12, 14, 36
	Recognise reflective symmetry in regular polygons: for example, know that a square has four axes of symmetry and an equilateral triangle has three Complete symmetrical patterns with two lines of symmetry at right angles (using squared paper or pegboard) Recognise where a shape will be after reflection in a mirror line parallel to one side (sides not all parallel or perpendicular to the mirror line) Recognise where a shape will be after a translation	3b: 20 4a: 25, 31 4b: 24, 31, 33
	Recognise positions and directions: read and plot co-ordinates in the first quadrant; **recognise perpendicular and parallel lines**	3b: 2, 14 4a: 14, 20, 38 4b: 26
	Understand and use angle measure in degrees Identify, estimate and order acute and obtuse angles Use a protractor to measure and draw acute and obtuse angles to the nearest 5° Calculate angles in a straight line	3b: 26 4b: 3 5: 2, 19

Yearly Teaching Programme: Year 6

Topics	Objectives	STEPS Teacher's Handbook Reference

■ Numbers and the number system

Topics	Objectives	STEPS Teacher's Handbook Reference
Place value, ordering and rounding	**Multiply and divide decimals mentally by 10 or 100, and integers by 1000, and explain the effect**	5: 22
	Use the vocabulary of estimation and approximation Consolidate rounding an integer to the nearest 10, 100 or 1000	4a: 1
	Find the difference between a positive and a negative integer, or two negatives integers, in a context such as temperature or the number line, and order a set of positive and negative integers	5: 4
Properties of numbers and number sequences	Recognise and extend number sequences, such as the sequence of square numbers, or the sequence of triangular numbers 1, 3, 6, 10, 15... Count on in steps of 0.1, 0.2, 0.25, 0.5..., and then back	5: 14, 35
	Make general statements about odd or even numbers, including the outcome of products	4b: 28
	Recognise multiples of 10×10. Know and apply simple tests of divisibility. Find simple common multiples	4b: 28
	Recognise squares of numbers to at least 12×12	5: 14
	Recognise prime numbers to at least 20 Factorise numbers to 100 into prime factors	5: 3
Fractions, decimals, percentages, ratio and proportion	Change a fraction such as $^{33}/_8$ to the equivalent mixed number $4^1/_8$, and vice versa Recognise relationships between fractions: for example, that $^1/_{10}$ is ten times $^1/_{100}$ and $^1/_{16}$ is half of $^1/_8$ **Reduce a fraction to its simplest form by cancelling common factors** in the numerator and denominator	5: 24, 26
	Order fractions such as $^2/_3$, $^3/_4$ and $^5/_6$ by converting them to fractions with a common denominator, and position them on a number line	Opportunities in 5: 24
	Use a fraction as an 'operator' to find fractions, including tenths and hundredths, **of numbers or quantities** (e.g. $^5/_8$ of 32, $^7/_{10}$ of 40, $^9/_{100}$ **of 400 centimetres)**	4b: 18
	Solve simple problems involving ratio and proportion	
	Use decimal notation for tenths and hundredths in calculations, and tenths, hundredths and thousandths when recording measurements Know what each digit represents in a number with up to three decimal places Give a decimal fraction lying between two others (e.g. between 3.4 and 3.5) **Order a mixed set of numbers** or measurements **with up to three decimal places**	4b: 29 5: 22, 24
	Round a number with two decimal places to the nearest tenth or to the nearest whole number	4a: 17
	Recognise the equivalence between the decimal and fraction forms of one half, one quarter, three quarters, one eighth... and tenths, hundredths and thousandths (e.g. $^{700}/_{1000} = ^{70}/_{100} = ^7/_{10} = 0.7$) Begin to convert a fraction to a decimal using division	5: 24

Topics	Objectives	STEPS Teacher's Handbook Reference
Fractions, decimals, percentages, ratio and proportion *continued*	**Understand percentage as the number of parts in every 100.** Express simple fractions such as one half, one quarter, three quarters, one third, two thirds..., and tenths and hundredths, as percentages (e.g. know that $\frac{1}{3} = 33\frac{1}{3}\%$) **Find simple percentages of small whole-number quantities** (e.g. find 10% of £500, then 20%, 40% and 80% by doubling)	5: 26

■ Calculations

Topics	Objectives	STEPS Teacher's Handbook Reference
Mental calculation strategies (+ and −)	Consolidate all strategies from previous year, including: find a difference by counting up; add or subtract the nearest multiple of 10, 100 or 1000, then adjust; use the relationship between addition and subtraction; add several numbers	**4b**: 7 **5**: 1, 13, 20, 25
	Use known number facts and place value to consolidate mental addition/subtraction (e.g. 470 + 380, 810 − 380, 7.4 + 9.8, 9.2 − 8.6)	
Pencil and paper procedures (+ and −)	Use informal pencil and paper methods to support, record or explain additions and subtractions **Extend written methods to column addition and subtraction of numbers involving decimals**	5: 13, 20
Understanding multiplication and division	Understand and use the relationships between the four operations, and the principles (not the names) of the arithmetic laws Use brackets	5: 9, 18
	Express a quotient as a fraction or as a decimal rounded to one decimal place. Divide £.p by a two-digit number to give £.p Round up or down after division, depending on the context	**4b**: 30
Rapid recall of multiplication and division facts	Consolidate knowing by heart: multiplication facts up to 10 × 10	5: 18
	Derive quickly: **division facts corresponding to tables up to 10 × 10;** squares of multiples of 10 to 100 (e.g. 60 × 60); doubles of two-digit numbers (e.g. 3.8 × 2, 0.76 × 2); doubles of multiples of 10 to 100 (e.g. 670 × 2); doubles of multiples of 100 to 10 000 (e.g. 6500 × 2); and the corresponding halves	5: 18
Mental calculation strategies (× and ÷)	Use related facts and doubling or halving. For example: double or halve the most significant digit first; to multiply by 25, multiply by 100 then divide by 4; double one number and halve the other; find the ×24 table by doubling the ×6 table twice	
	Use factors (e.g. 35 × 18 = 35 × 6 × 3)	Opportunities in **5**: 18
	Use closely related facts: for example, multiply by 49 or 51 by multiplying by 50 and adjusting Develop the ×17 table by adding facts from the ×10 and ×7 tables	Opportunities in **5**: 18
	Partition (e.g. 87 × 6 = (80 × 6) + (7 × 6); 3.4 × 3 = (3 × 3) + (0.4 × 3)).	Opportunities in **5**: 18
	Use the relationship between multiplication and division	5: 25
	Use known number facts and place value to consolidate mental multiplication and division	5: 22

Topics	Objectives	STEPS Teacher's Handbook Reference
Pencil and paper procedures (× and ÷)	Approximate first. Use informal pencil and paper methods to support, record or explain multiplications and divisions **Extend written methods to:** multiplication of ThHTU × U (short multiplication); **short multiplication of numbers involving decimals;** **long multiplication of a three-digit by a two-digit integer;** short division of TU or HTU by U (mixed-number answer); division of HTU by TU (long division, whole-number answer); **short division of numbers involving decimals**	5: 7, 9, 18, 22, 30
Using a calculator	Develop calculator skills and use a calculator effectively	Integral throughout
Checking results of calculations	Check with the inverse operation when using a calculator	5: 9, 20, 25
	Check the sum of several numbers by adding in reverse order	
	Check with an equivalent calculation	5: 9, 18
	Estimate by approximating (round to nearest 10, 100 or 1000), then check result	Opportunities in **4b**: 25
	Use knowledge of sums, differences, products of odd/even numbers	**4b**: 28
	Use tests of divisibility	

■ Solving problems

Making decisions	Choose and use appropriate number operations to solve problems, and appropriate ways of calculating: mental, mental with jottings, written methods, calculator	Opportunities throughout number sections (blue) in STEPS 4b and 5
Reasoning and generalising about numbers or shapes	Explain methods and reasoning, orally and in writing	5: 3, 9, 13, 18
	Solve mathematical problems or puzzles, recognise and explain patterns and relationships, generalise and predict Suggest extensions asking 'What if...?'	5: 3, 9, 13, 18, 20, 25
	Make and investigate a general statement about familiar numbers or shapes by finding examples that satisfy it Develop from explaining a generalised relationship in words to expressing it in a formula using letters as symbols (e.g. the cost of n articles at 15p each)	4b: 17, 23 5: 1, 13, 17, 18, 25
Problems involving 'real life', money or measures	**Identify and use appropriate operations (including combinations of operations) to solve word problems involving numbers and quantities** based on 'real life', money or measures (including time), using one or more steps, including converting pounds to foreign currency, or vice versa, and calculating percentages such as VAT **Explain methods and reasoning**	Opportunities throughout all sections in STEPS 4b and 5 including 5: 30 (money); 5: 33 (time) 5: 26 (percentages)

■ Handling data

Handling data	Use the language associated with probability to discuss events, including those with equally likely outcomes	5: 12
	Solve a problem by representing, **extracting and interpreting data in tables, graphs, charts** and diagrams, including those generated by a computer, for example: line graphs (e.g. for distance/time, for a multiplication table, a conversion graph, a graph of pairs of numbers adding to 8); frequency tables and bar charts with grouped discrete data (e.g. test marks 0–5, 6–10, 11–15...)	5: 11, 12, 15, 23

Topics	Objectives	STEPS Teacher's Handbook Reference
Handling data *continued*	Find the mode and range of a set of data Begin to find the median and mean of a set of data	5: 15

■ Measures, shape and space

Measures	Use, read and write standard metric units (km, m, cm, mm, kg, g, l, ml, cl), including their abbreviations and relationships between them Convert smaller to larger units (e.g. m to km, cm or mm to m, g to kg, ml to l) and vice versa Know imperial units (mile, pint, gallon, lb, oz) Know rough equivalents of lb and kg, oz and g, miles and km, litres and pints or gallons	**4b:** 29, 32 **5:** 5, 10, 17, 28, 31, 34
	Suggest suitable units and measuring equipment to estimate or measure length, mass or capacity Record estimates and readings from scales to a suitable degree of accuracy	**4b:** 29, 32 **5:** 5, 10, 17, 28, 31, 34
	Calculate the perimeter and area of simple compound shapes that can be split into rectangles	**4b:** 17, 23 **5:** 10, 17, 34
	Appreciate the different times around the world	
Shape and space	Describe and visualise properties of solid shapes such as parallel or perpendicular faces or edges Classify quadrilaterals, using criteria such as parallel sides, equal angles, equal sides...	**4a:** 12, 28 **4b:** 33 **5:** 21
	Make shapes with increasing accuracy. Visualise 3-D shapes from 2-D drawings and identify different nets for a closed cube	**4b:** 6, 10, 12, 14, 33 **5:** 8, 19, 21, 32
	Recognise where a shape will be after reflection: in a mirror line touching the shape at a point (sides of shape not necessarily parallel or perpendicular to the mirror line); in two mirror lines at right angles (sides of shape all parallel or perpendicular to the mirror line) Recognise where a shape will be after two translations	**5:** 16, 27
	Read and plot co-ordinates in all four quadrants	**5:** 16, 29
	Recognise and estimate angles **Use a protractor to measure** and draw **acute and obtuse angles to the nearest degree** Check that the sum of the angles of a triangle is 180°, for example, by measuring or paper folding Calculate angles in a triangle or around a point Recognise where a shape will be after a rotation through 90° about one of its vertices	**4b:** 3, 24 **5:** 2, 6, 19, 29